The Discipline
&
Culture of Innovation

For free information on all our
publications, please register at:

www.profiteditorial.com

or send us an e-mail to:
info@profiteditorial.com

Follow us on:

 @profiteditorial

 Profit Editorial

 Editorial Profit

Jay Rao & Fran Chuan

The Discipline & Culture of Innovation

A Socratic Journey

«Any form of reproduction, distribution, communication to the public or transformation of this work may only be performed with authorisation from its copyright holders, unless exempt by law. Should you need to photocopy or scan an excerpt of this work, please contact CEDRO (Centro Español de Derechos Reprográficos) (www.conlicencia.com; 91 702 19 70 / 93 272 04 45)».

© Jay Rao & Fran Chuán, 2013

© Profit Editorial, 2013 (www.profiteditorial.com)
Profit Editorial I., S.L., 2013

Cover Design: XicArt
Print Design: www.eximpre.com

ISBN: 978-84-15735-61-8
Printed by: Gráficas Rey, S.L.

I dedicate this book to my wife Clemencia and our children Maya and Paloma. They endure without complaints my frequent and at times extended travels for teaching and talking engagements. Without their absolute affection and significant sacrifices this book would not have been possible. I am also grateful to my parents, my sister, and my extended family for their enthusiastic encouragement, constant cheer leading, loads of love and an unwavering belief in all things that I do.

JAY RAO, BOSTON

Only self-confidence and conversation with others move us to explore new worlds and new opportunities. I have only words of gratitude for Anna, my wife, for her patient response to the continuous challenges in which I, as an entrepreneur and innovator, involve her. And for her patient and inestimable contributions through the innumerable drafts that this text went through before it reached your hands.

FRAN CHUAN, BARCELONA

Contents

	Page
Dedication	5
Preface	9
Introduction	11
Chapter 1: The Desire for Change	27
Chapter 2: Innovation is Different	33
Chapter 3: Discipline of Innovation	49
Chapter 4: The Practice and Dynamics of Innovation . . .	65
Chapter 5: The Culture of Innovation	81
Chapter 6: Starting the Journey	101

Preface

The word "innovation" is fashionable. Everyone uses it, and it has become the magic solution to all our social and economic problems.

We witness a great proliferation of attempts to continuously make our society and our production systems more innovative, creating Ministries of Innovation, launching public support programs to R&D and Innovation, and organizing events and symposia to facilitate exchanging ideas. We even compare ourselves with successful companies looking for which traits to imitate.

In many occasions however, the results are appalling. Despite significant resources devoted to this effort, the expected transformation does not happen as desired.

I believe that in many cases the problem lies in our lack of clarity about the real meaning of the word "innovation": some think in R&D, others in radical change or in organizational restructuring, and many do not even take the time to form an opinion on the subject, being too busy with their daily tasks.

In an entertaining way, we will find some clues throughout the book to help us define INNOVATION more precisely, and clarify that it is not a process, but a result which translates into new products, services, business opportunities, markets, etc.

All organizations have an Innovation Department or something similar, but throughout my professional career, always linked to the world of innovation in different companies, I have discovered that the equation INNOVATION = RESULTS is what makes the difference between the innovative and the non-innovative companies.

The innovative companies focus on the expected results to be delivered by the resources invested on innovation, developing the tools necessary to achieve them, but never the other way round.

The innovative companies act, practice, and fail – or sometimes succeed. I like the statistics showing that more than 90% of innovations fail, because it means that a significant percentage of them are successful. Let's not forget that when we implement an innovative product, service or business, our competitive advantage will be a more powerful force than any other management tool at our reach. Is it worth? I believe so.

I hope that you enjoy the book as much as I did: the dialogues, the paper towels, Mike the "Socratic" master and John his gifted pupil. If you start reading it, you will be rewarded with the initial clues allowing you to start the innovation journey, … neither more nor less; a journey we all agree we don't know where it will take us, but in any case always stimulating …

AGUSTIN DELGADO MARTIN
Director of Innovation
IBERDROLA

P. S. I immensely enjoy my journeys of adventure, but I always get myself prepared in advance.

Introduction

Innovation. It may be the business buzzword of our time. Corporate ads and annual reports proclaim that "Innovation is what we are all about." CEOs exhort their people to "Be more innovative." Meager product alterations are touted as innovations. "Now available in five unique colors!" Chief Innovation Officers are being appointed in more and more organizations.

Yet for all the use and abuse of the term, few firms have demonstrated an ability to innovate repeatedly and in meaningful ways over time. For the rest, *innovation* is more of a slogan or aspiration than a practice that produces dependable results. Most employees recognize this; they've managed to separate the hype from reality.

The word *innovation* has become popularized to the point of overuse and tedium, why do we still leave innovation to chance and good fortune? Why do we go on confusing innovation with just invention and R&D? Even organizations that have seriously committed to innovation are only achieving partial results because of their over reliance on idea generation software and premature use of rigid stage-gate processes. In fact, on

Dec. 31st 2008, Bruce Nussbaum, *BusinessWeek's* ex-Innovation guru wrote:

> "Innovation died in 2008, killed off by overuse, misuse, narrowness, incrementalism and failure to evolve. It was done in by CEOs, consultants, marketeers, advertisers and business journalists who degraded and devalued the idea by conflating it with change, technology, design, globalization, trendiness, and anything 'new.' It was done in by an obsession with measurement, metrics and math and a demand for predictability in an unpredictable world."

Four years later, this overuse and misuse was still alive and well. A May 23rd, 2012 article from the Wall Street Journal, "You call that innovation?" validated and reinforced this observation. Below were a few highlights from the article that was based on a CapGemini Study of 260 Global executives: (1) 4 in 10 have a Chief Innovation Officer and such titles may be mainly "for appearances," and (2) most of them conceded their companies still don't have a clear innovation strategy to support the role.

Every year I find myself in front of one-thousand-plus executives and senior managers, and hundreds of executive MBA students, and I ask them the same question: "How many of you are tired of the word *innovation*?" Many hands go up. When asked why, their responses are predictable:

> "There's a lot of talk about innovation around here but very little action."

> "We're asked to be innovative, but are never given the time or resources."

> "Our innovative projects are shelved whenever quarterly targets are missed."

> "The term is meaningless—anything that's slightly out of the ordinary around here is touted as an innovation."

> "Our leaders want us to be innovative when they aren't."

The overuse and abuse of the term *innovation* is leading to dismal outcomes and disillusionment. It is also wasting lots of money. Some firms invest in group collaborative software and creative spaces and go-to-market new product development systems. Still others set up internal venture funds and innovation tournaments in order to capture creative ideas. And, of course, lots of money is spent on consultants who, it is hoped, will whisper the secret formula of innovation into the CEO's ear. This spending, however, hasn't paid off as hoped.

On the other hand, as technology cycles come faster, as the amount of information explodes exponentially from month to month, and as competition appears from unexpected corners of the globe, serious executives are increasingly hoping that "Innovation" can keep their enterprises competitive and thriving. They are asking tough questions. They are earnest about their investments in innovation. They are trying to solve difficult problems and their firms are creating new value for their customers. There is data to show that innovation does pay off.

So, innovation efforts are delivering for some firms and not for others. This book explains why.

The Book in a Nutshell

Innovation in enterprises results from two co-existing conditions: (1) *treating innovation as a discipline*, and (2) *creating a culture of innovation*. Executives have the power to create each of these essential conditions. They needn't rely on luck—though luck never hurts. And they needn't rely on a strategy of hope—which is no strategy at all. Discipline and a culture that supports innovation will produce the growth that these executives so badly desire.

Some empirical evidence on Innovation

Contrary to conventional wisdom, an extensive 2004 Booz Allen Hamilton Global Innovation study of 1000 publicly held firms around the world that spent the most on R&D showed that R&D spending levels had no impact on sales growth, gross profit, operating profit, enterprise profit, market capitalization, or total shareholder return.[1] Booz Allen also investigated the relationship between R&D and patents. Firms that spent a lot on R&D did have a much larger patent portfolio, but the level of patent activity did not correlate to growth, profitability and shareholder return. The same study also concluded that of all the core functions of most companies, innovation still has the most competitive value, but was managed with the least discipline.

A 2007 McKinsey innovation report[2], based on a survey of nearly 1400 executives from around the world concluded the following:

- Senior executives cited innovation as an important driver of growth but few explicitly lead and managed it
- CEOs and Executives were frustrated with their efforts to jumpstart innovation initiatives
- There was overall dissatisfaction with the dismal outcomes of their innovation efforts
- Mimicking best practices were often ineffective
- Resources and Processes that were applied were either underutilized or not achieving scale to have a financial impact
- 94% of the executives responded that people and corporate culture were the most important drivers of innovation
- Nearly a third of them managed innovation on an ad hoc basis.

Another 2007 McKinsey survey of 600 executives revealed that senior executives did not actively encourage and model innovative behaviors. The Booz study had also concluded similarly about the importance of R&D spending along with certain approaches to organization, culture and decision making.

---

1 Money Isn't Everything, S+B, Booz Allen Hamilton, Dec. 5, 2005
2 Leadership and Innovation, The McKinsey Quarterly, 2008, No. 1

In 2010, a multi-year study by the Boston Consulting Group consistently found that focusing on innovation did pay off; there was a strong correlation between innovation prowess and overall business performance. BCG found that true innovators outperformed their peers by nearly 12.4% over a three year period and by a modest 2% over ten years.[3] In the same report, 71% of the nearly 1500 executives and managers felt that innovation was among the top three priorities for the firm. However, despite some improvement over a four year period, dissatisfaction among executives with the financial return on innovation spending remained high (45% of 1590 respondents from around the world). But the dissatisfaction among employees was much higher (nearly 64%).

The previously mentioned 2004 Booz Allen study had identified from among the Global 1000 largest R&D spenders only a small set of 94 so-called high-leverage innovators had chalked up five consecutive years of above median performance in terms of growth, profit and shareholder value while spending less than their peer group for their innovation initiatives. In 2009, 2010 and 2011 Booz Allen studies of the Global 1000 largest R&D spenders, the Top 10 Most Innovative Firms (as identified by their executive respondents) had consistently and significantly outperformed not only their industry peers but also the top 10 R&D spenders on three financial metrics – revenue growth, EBITA as a percentage of revenues and market cap growth.[4][5][6]

---

3 Innovation 2010, *BCG Report*, Boston Consulting Group, April 2010
4 "The Global Innovation 1000, How the Top Innovators Keep Winning," *Strategy + Business*, Booz & Co., issue 61, winter 2010
5 "The Global Innovation 1000, Why Culture is Key," *Strategy + Business*, Booz & Co., issue 65, winter 2011
6 "The Global Innovation 1000, Making Ideas Work," *Strategy + Business*, Booz & Co., issue 69, Winter 2012

What is causing the pain?

There are several reasons as to why Innovation is not working for even those who are serious and investing in earnest. Certainly, with so many people thinking and talking about innovation, we must be making some progress. Perhaps. But imagine for a moment how much *more* progress we could be making if innovation was treated less as a buzzword or aspiration, and more as a true management *discipline*!

I am a professor of management at Babson College, where my focus is innovation and corporate entrepreneurship. Over the last decade I have worked closely with more than 40 firms around the world—small, medium, and huge multinationals (a complete list of these firms can be found on my website). My work takes the form of speeches, seminars, executive education, and consulting. I constantly hear the horror stories related to innovation initiatives and efforts inside of these firms.

In our own experience, it is not just the majority of the large, global 1000 firms that are struggling with innovation. Innovation naiveté is still rampant among executives, managers and employees in firms of all sizes. A lot has been written and talked about Innovation. Yet myths persist. Typical myths include:

- Innovation is invention
- Innovation is just for the R&D folk
- Innovation is technology
- Innovation is just about products
- Innovation is new product development
- Innovation does not work in my industry
- Innovation does not work in my country
- Innovation is luck
- Innovation is expensive

- Innovation is about giving everyone 10% time off to do their own thing
- Innovation happens when we buy an idea generating software
- Innovation is a process, so let us implement a funnel like stage gate.

These are not just myths. This is illiteracy. It is not just the term that is misused and overused, the concept of innovation is misconceived. And, it's about time that we address this ignorance. To put it simply, **Innovation is a Discipline! Period.**

What do we mean by this? Mr. Nussbaum was both right and wrong. The faddish Innovation 1.0 is dead but the systematic Innovation 2.0 is still in its infancy. Currently, in a majority of the firms, Innovation is not being treated as a management discipline like the other management disciplines—strategy, marketing, finance, economics, IT. Yes, innovation has become mainstream, but the way it is put into action in most firms is still not disciplined—deliberate and determined. Innovation can be a systematically planned and organized activity and with a certain degree of predictability. In terms of its maturity, the discipline and the general practice of innovation today is where the practice and discipline of quality was 20 years ago.

To understand this, it may be instructive to look at how other management disciplines evolved over time.

Evolution of Management Disciplines

Many disciplines operate in the world of business, and their evolutions provide insights into the development of innovation as a field of practice. Consider the very established discipline of marketing. In 1905, University of Pennsylvania offered a course in "The Marketing of Products." Like other disciplines, marketing has several conceptual frameworks (like the "4Ps") and a unique vocabulary. It has developed practical methods (e.g., segmentation) and tools (e.g., conjoint analysis) that practitioners master through formal study and apply in a variety of situations. Subfields of marketing such as advertising and consumer behavior have broadened the discipline. Over time, academic departments have formed to increase the body of marketing knowledge and to pass it on to others. Journals, professional associations, and conferences dedicated to marketing and its application have emerged over the years.

We have witnessed a similar evolution with the 'quality' movement which, like innovation today, was initially more aspirational than effective. Let us look at how the quality movement emerged, developed, and embedded itself in practice and into enterprise culture.

The quality movement has gone through several phases of maturity in its 50-year history: beginning with Deming's 14 points, moving on to Juran's trilogy, then to Feigenbaum's TQC, to TQM and most recently Six Sigma.

Post-World War II, Dr. Deming and Juran taught statistical and quality management techniques to Japanese businesses. By the late 1960s, Japanese management had fully embraced Total Quality Control. The focus at that time was inspection, reaction to defects and quality control. Through the 70s, the responsibility for quality was very much functional and limited to a few people in the firm. Still, this enabled the Japanese to enter the U.S. markets with cheaper products and higher levels of quality. It was only after significant market share losses in several industries—steel, home appliances, automotive, memory chips—did the U.S. and W. European firms acknowledge the importance of quality management.

The adoption of quality practices weren't limited to business applications. In 1980 the U.S. Naval Air Systems introduced the term TQM. The new thinking included—design-in quality, prevention of defects and everyone responsible for quality.

Because many commercial vendors worked with Air System command, this fostered awareness and adoption among many companies. We saw many companies embrace TQM and it spread like wildfire. But, initiatives at a large number of firms failed due to poor education, sloppy implementation, and ineffective change management practices.

Six Sigma marked the latest evolution in the quality movement. While retaining several fundamental statistical and process principles from before, it was a more deliberate, systematic and comprehensive approach that clearly represented a major step forward compared to previous generations. Developed in the mid-1980s at Motorola, Six Sigma rose to prominence when Motorola won the Malcolm Baldrige National Quality Award in 1988; the first year the award was presented. Six Sigma had a few distinctive features that its predecessors lacked—(1) it integrated with existing strategy and initiatives of the firm, (2) it was driven and championed by top leaders in the firm, (3) it created a cadre of experts—master black-belts—in the concepts and tools of quality, (4) it trained an entire community—black and green belts—to become knowledgeable about its strategic implications, and (5) this community had the ability to use the principles of quality in specific situations by way of focused projects and apply proven change management skills.

This practical, comprehensive approach helped the critical principles and practice of quality to percolate into a majority of firms worldwide. Simultaneously, the quality movement evolved to become a "discipline," i.e., a body of knowledge or a field of study.

So, like all academic disciplines – physics, sociology, linguistics, accounting, marketing, quality – innovation too can be managed. It can be taught, it can be learned, it can be practiced and over time enterprises can master innovation.

We can learn several lessons from how firms have mastered other disciplines like marketing and quality.

Mastering a Discipline

Mastery is the result of desire, choice and commitment.

Firms cannot excel at any discipline unless there is a burning desire to do so from the leadership team. If there is the desire then the executives will spend time and money towards building capabilities within the enterprise to master that discipline. To master a discipline is a choice. Not all firms are great at marketing. Not all firms choose to be great at operational excellence or for that matter at consistently developing great leaders. Hence, to excel at innovation is also a choice. Nobody is forcing firms to be great at innovation; especially not the firm's competitors. So, the leaders have to make a wholehearted commitment to excel at it.

Mastery requires a cadre of experts to lead the way.

Not everyone in the firm is a finance expert. Not everyone in the firm is a HR expert. Hence, not everyone in the firm will want to be an innovation expert. Yet, like how enterprises created six-sigma masters and experts internally, firms need to create a similar cadre of innovation experts. Very few firms have developed these internal experts in innovation. We need to remember that having a great R&D group does not automatically result in innovation.

Mastery requires a broad-based understanding of principles and methods.

While most inventions come from individuals or small groups of 2 or 3 people, a vast majority of innovations are a result of a community effort. Hence broad knowledge about the *lingua franca of innovation*—principles, frameworks, concepts and tools—enterprise wide is imperative. Today, in most enterprises we expect all employees to have some rudimentary knowledge or skill in the concepts and tools of all major management disciplines – finance, marketing, operations etc. Innovation is no different. Unfortunately, this does not exist in most firms today.

Mastery requires years of effort.

It takes years to master any discipline. You master a discipline through discipline (purposeful practice, rigor, patience and perseverance). Fortunately, the journey to master any discipline is the same: Knowledge → Practice → Discipline. There are no short cuts and no magic bullets. Yet, in reality I regularly encounter executives that expect employees to be magically innovative without any formal training and/or practice.

Mastering any discipline is like mastering a language. Most of us are quite happy to acquire conversational skills in a second language and rarely try to gain expertise. Similarly, most firms are quick to learn a few of the foundational skills of innovation. But it is not sufficient to set them apart in the competitive landscape. However, mastery and expertise in innovation is still a rarity among enterprises.

Mastery requires both Discipline and Culture

Executives who are genuine and serious about innovation are asking serious questions: "How do you innovate? How do you invest in R&D? What processes do you set up in the firm for innovation? How can we measure innovation?" These are necessary questions; but, not sufficient. Unfortunately, one cannot make people creative and innovative. The only thing executives can do is to create a climate where people can be naturally creative. So, at the heart of innovation is the corporate culture.

Innovation is a social science like marketing, leadership and psychology. While accounting, finance, and IT are formal sciences that are governed by logic and rules. Physical or life sciences obey the laws of nature. However, in social sciences there are no rules or laws. Social sciences have general principles, frameworks, tools, concepts etc. Unfortunately, thus far, several executives and firms have been approaching innovation as though it is a formal science like quality and/or physical science like biology or chemistry. So, firms are still using the wrong tools, wrong techniques and wrong resources to manage innovation. Further, in several industries, innovation is narrowly defined as R&D and invention. This directly leads these firms to take very structured approaches towards innovation that eschews all the creative, artistic and humanistic elements that are central to innovation in general. All of this is leading to all the poor results and frustration.

The previously mentioned 2007 McKinsey innovation report, based on a survey of nearly 1400 executives from around the world showed that 94% of the executives agreed that *people* and *corporate culture* were the most important drivers of innovation. In another major study of 759 firms across 17 major economies, "Corporate Culture" was found to be the primary driver of radical innovation[7]. Booz Allen has been surveying the Global 1000 firms and reporting on them since 2005. In their 2011 report[8], they concluded:

> "The elements that make up a truly innovative company are many: a focused innovation strategy, a winning overall business strategy, deep customer insight, great talent, and the right set of capabilities to achieve successful execution. More important than any of the individual elements, however, is the role played by corporate culture — the organization's self-sustaining patterns of behaving, feeling, thinking, and believing — in tying them all together."

Unfortunately, the same study revealed that only about half the responding firms said that their corporate culture robustly supports their innovation strategy. Further, about the same proportion said that their innovation strategy was aligned with their corporate strategy.

Treating innovation as a discipline is necessary but not sufficient. However, approaching innovation as a discipline in combination with a culture of innovation is an unbeatable combination.

---

[7] Radical Innovation Across Nations: The Preeminence of Corporate Culture, Journal of Marketing, Jan. 2009

[8] The Global Innovation 1000, Why Culture is Key, Issue 65, Winter 2011

Who will benefit from reading this book?

Executives who accept this book's central message will stop annoying employees and shareholders with empty rhetoric about "being innovative" and begin building a solid, manageable discipline of innovation within their enterprises.

Once they read this book, you'll recognize that creative ideas, resources, processes, and metrics are just parts of a broader discipline called innovation that can be taught, learned, practiced, perfected and predicted.

Any enterprise that benefits from genuine innovation—in the development of physical products, services, or in the improvement of internal process—can benefit from the central thesis of this book. Companies that have mastered the discipline of quality and continuous improvement may get the most from it.

This book will also help executives that already deem innovation as important, but do not know how to get started on "the journey" towards creating a "culture of innovation." It will also help those who have already started the journey, but are not getting the results that they were expecting.

Layout of the book

At this stage, if you still wish to continue reading this book, it is laid out as described below.

The rest of the book is written as a dialog between a professor at a reputed business school and a skeptical executive. The dialog offers a simple and systematic approach for learning several fundamental concepts of innovation and answers numerous questions that executives usually harbor as they are exploring new management fads and are contemplating embarking on a new journey of navigating change within the firm.

As Edward Deming said, survival is not mandatory. Similarly, nobody is forcing a firm to be innovative. So, innovation is a choice. If chosen as a strategic competitive weapon, innovation has to be approached with the same intentional fervor as any major management initiative – Strategic Planning, ERP implementation or Six-Sigma. But still most executives believe that it is a peripheral activity or a luxury. So, in each chapter of this book are key leadership questions, decisions and choices that the executive reader will be forced to ponder and reflect upon.

The following paragraphs briefly cover the main takeaway from each of the book chapters.

Chapter 1 – The Desire for Change

Chapter 1 describes an executive that is plagued with a feeling of helplessness because the future prospects for the enterprise he runs are not promising. While the executive is convinced that what made the firm successful to this day is not what is going to make them successful going forward, he is quite unsure as to how he can break out of the status quo.

Chapter 2 – Innovation is Different

Chapter 2 points to one of the fundamental differences between innovation and all other management philosophies that have preceded it and those that were wholeheartedly embraced and adopted by most businesses. Specifically, clear distinctions are made between the concepts of quality and innovation and between incremental and radical innovation.

Chapter 3 – The Discipline of Innovation

Chapter 3 delves into the fact that innovation is a *discipline*. It is a body of knowledge like any other – quality, finance, marketing, bio-chemistry etc. Most importantly like all disciplines, innovation can be managed as a deliberate, comprehensive and strategic management function. So, it is not magic. It is not luck. Fortunately, the journey an enterprise has to undertake to master any management discipline is the same. This journey consists of three steps: Knowledge, Practice and Perserverance.

Chapter 4 – the Practice and Dynamics of Innovation

Chapter 4 delves into the practice and dynamics of innovation. All innovation happens in a community and the fundamental basis for the superior performance of any community is a common language. Every discipline—medicine, chemistry, law—has its own *lingua franca*. Each *lingua franca* has its own structure, its own principles, concepts and tools. So does Innovation. The first step to create a community of innovators is to teach them the *lingua franca* of innovation. Only then can the community be able to practice and master the discipline of innovation. This chapter also makes clear distinctions between the concepts of risk, uncertainty and ambiguity and how firms should approach and manage their portfolio of innovation projects based on those differences.

Chapter 5 – The Culture of Innovation

Chapter 5 outlines the journey of creating a culture of innovation within the firm. The creation of a true and pervasive culture of innovation in an enterprise, department or team, will bear multiple fruits. This chapter introduces the 6 fundamental foundation blocks that firms have to build to implement a culture of innovation—Values, Behaviors, Climate, Resources, Processes and definition of Success.

Chapter 6 – Starting the Journey

Chapter 6 looks at our current understanding about how *learning* happens. Innovation is about continuously learning and uncovering the "unknown." We look at how individuals learn and how firms learn. This chapter describes the limits of existing knowledge and how current knowledge limits a firm's ability to learn. Finally, in this chapter we assert that firms will die when they stop learning.

Acknowledgements

The contents of this book have been very heavily influenced by the following great thinkers, practitioners, executives, academics and consultants: Peter Drucker, Edward Deming, Jiddu Krishnamurthy, Clayton Christensen, Jim Collins, Gary Hamel, Daniel Pink, Abraham Maslow, Ken Blanchard, Geoffrey Moore, Jim Utterback, Jon Katzenbach, and Edgar Schein.

It has also been greatly shaped by numerous discussions with our colleagues and friends Neal Thornberry, Joe Weintraub, JB Kassarjian, Jean-Pierre Jeannette, Sebastian Fixson, Len Schlesinger, Allan Cohen, Les Charm, Ed Marram, Alberto Gimeno, Ivor Morgan, Anirudh Dhebar, Jim Watkinson and Richard Luecke.

We wish you luck and lots of discipline.

Enjoy *The Journey*!

Chapter 1

The Desire for Change

The view John had from his roomy office was relaxing and, on that day, bright and motivating. Spring always seemed stimulating to him, with its clear, warm days. From his third floor window he could see the crowns of the trees in the spacious garden that surrounded the company building. The view of the garden was serene, and at the same time the ferment that was typical of the season could be seen: flowers budding everywhere, the new, brilliant green foliage, birds fluttering around.

He also felt the ferment, and now he could see before him the opportunity to start the change that he'd been contemplating for months. But... had the right moment arrived? Were they ready to take on this new challenge? In fact, over the past weeks his view of the capabilities of his organization had been altered; he couldn't allow things to continue as they had until now. But the loneliness of the leader moved him to wonder whether his team would follow him in this adventure on which—in truth—he had already embarked.

As the chief executive of a service company, John had often reflected on why an enterprise of several hundred employees was bogged down in its offerings and, although they weren't doing badly, growth had stagnated. In previous downturns he used to have a somewhat rough idea that the growth would come back when the economy turned. But this time he wasn't sure that the customers would be coming back.

John felt that he was well networked and thus had a keen pulse on business trends. In addition to meeting current and prospective customers regularly he attended management forums, conferences and seminars. In the encounters with other executives, talk often turned to the lack of energy and novelty in organizations; the "same old, same old" really seemed to be a widespread phenomenon. But this "normality" was no excuse—the lack of ability to innovate in his own enterprise—to stop worrying him.

In past periods of economic buoyancy, most managers agreed that the time was right to make the most of star products or services. Almost no one spoke of changing things, adhering to the slogan "don't touch a system that works". Now it was different; things weren't going so well, everything had become more complex, and many already spoke of the need to innovate to survive, but they still agreed on the need to contain spending, if not to reduce it, to balance accounts and to internationalize to spread the risk. But few put their desire to innovate into action! Those who achieved success with their initiatives were even fewer. Why weren't some of the most renowned firms—lead by executives that he really respected—not succeeding even after spending a lot of money and effort into what they called innovation related activities. What disturbed him most was that he didn't even consider a lot of what they were doing as being innovative.

John wasn't satisfied with the way things were going and, although the company he managed was riding out the crisis with a certain dignity, he wasn't at ease; he couldn't see a clear future for his organization. They would survive but definitely not prevail.

His suppositions were confirmed on the day when, during a quarterly closing management committee meeting, the figures presented for the quarter that just ended confirmed what was coming. Sales had stagnated and, given the market situation, they'd had to lower prices and lengthen collection times, with the resulting negative impact on margins. And the projections didn't indicate any improvement in the immediate future. Something had to be done!

He asked the committee members to meet again in two weeks, and requested that each one contribute an idea—with supporting arguments—for actions they could put in motion in the short- and medium term to improve what was clearly a negative trend.

After adjourning the committee meeting, John returned to his office. After a few minutes Emma, his assistant, came in to hand him the three usual work folders: the week's appointments, matters to be dealt with and the incoming mail.

John was in the habit of having a look at all the mail that came to him; he knew that the great majority would go into the trash after he'd read the first few lines, but he believed that sometimes opportunities or interesting items arrived that one can't immediately throw out.

And that's what happened on this occasion. One by one he was going through letters, promotional brochures, industry newsletters and invitations to conferences and seminars, winnowing out the pieces that interested him. Until, a leaflet caught his eye announcing a seminar to be given by a well-known business school. Its title was "Innovation in Action" and it raised a series of assertions and suggestive questions: on failures in innovation initiatives, on the difference between risk and uncertainty, on knowledge impeding learning, on the great gap between thought and action...and ended by proposing that innovation shouldn't be a destination, but rather a journey to create a culture of innovation. What really caught his attention was a statement that said, "We help managers learn to fail and celebrate failure." He circled this sentence and the words "culture of innovation" with his pen.

He made some more notes on the leaflet and put it into a folder in which he reserved potentially interesting documents for a time. From time to time he would review the contents of this folder, throwing away everything that had lost the magic that had inspired him to save it.

Two weeks later, John and his management committee team came together again in the meeting room to hold the session on proposals for improvements. His expectations were high; he had a cohesive, hardworking team; surely among all the ideas that they presented, there would be some that would generate actions with an impact on the organization.

One by one the committee members presented the ideas they had developed with their respective teams. In many cases, the contributions stimulated lively debate, but most of the ideas were oriented to reducing costs and improving efficiency, or to launching marketing or sales campaigns to strengthen the services the company already offered. As the session went on, John leaned further and further back in his chair as his concern increased. When the debate generated by the last speaker had ended, John spoke.

> "I want to thank you for the good effort you've put in with your teams, both in preparing your case and in the defense of your ideas during the debates. I think this meeting has been very informative for all of us, and I'm convinced that, with the execution of the actions that we've agreed to set in motion, our situation will improve." John paused. "However, when that moment arrives, how do you think we'll be different from today?"

The meeting room was silent for a few seconds. Then the executives began discussing the question among themselves. John waited patiently until one of them expressed the overall conclusion.

> "We'll really be more efficient, and we will have straightened out the trend we saw in the last quarter closing, but we won't be different. In any event, we'll be better."

The room was still silent. By now, the executive team knew the pensive John very well. Some in the room had worked with him for more than a decade. As the chief executive he had patted their back for their work. But as a friend and colleague—and many in the room considered him just that—he would bring them back to reality to push them to the next level.

> "Aha! We'll be better, but for how long? How many times will we be able to do this exercise until we can no longer reduce costs or launch more campaigns? Let me ask a few more questions. Why haven't we seen, in the great ideas presented today, anything that will make us different? Are we creating something different in the long run, are we being truly innovative?"

Another executive broke the silence that had fallen over the group again, and said, "We really can't say that we're an innovative organization. For all these years we've been offering our customers what they need, and we have a very substantial portfolio of satisfied customers."

John accepted the comment with good grace and, after a few moments of reflection, one of the phrases from the leaflet he'd put away a few weeks ago crossed his mind: they conceived innovation as a result of culture, a culture which—his executive was right—they lacked.

He thanked his colleagues for their work and encouraged them to put the improvement actions they'd agreed to into practice.

More importantly he challenged them to think and reflect as to how the firm could do things differently and/or different things rather than just doing the same things better.

John returned to his office, pulled out the folder of temporarily interesting subjects and found the leaflet that he'd put away days ago on the innovation seminar. He reread it and found that it focused precisely on the subject that concerned him: "Innovation in Action". He carefully read the details of the program, its contents, length, format and dates. He consulted his calendar and didn't see anything that couldn't be postponed that would stand in the way of him attending a four-day seminar. Having attended several such programs in the past, he was skeptical. Most had not impressed him.

The situation of the company he managed would probably improve with the actions that were going to be set in motion, but something more had to be done. "When was the last innovation made in this enterprise? Even in their industry?" he asked himself. He couldn't even remember! What troubled him most was the fact that even if they, by chance, had a new hit product or service in the next one year; that wouldn't be enough. The firm would need a string of these to prevail in the long run. He wasn't sure, but he somehow felt that it might be something to do with the firm's culture.

> "Damn! I won't lose anything by attending and devoting a little of my time to discovering other perspectives. With just one or two ideas that I can apply to my day-to-day activity, the experience may be worthwhile," he thought. If nothing, he wanted to get away from the office for a while to clear his mind.

He called Emma and asked her to register him for the seminar. He realized that the seminar was a little over a month away, and that gave him enough time to put out some more day-to-day fires.

Chapter 2

Innovation is Different!

Monday was reserved for the participants' arrival. The conference center was a couple of hours drive from John's city, in a big old rambling house surrounded by nature. There was a small apartment building annex—with all the executive amenities—for the residents. John had not set high expectations for this program, but he was grateful for the fact that it was residential. It enabled him to isolate himself from the day-to-day concerns that drove his life to such a great extent. Irrespective of how the seminar would be, he knew that he would benefit from the readings, meeting other executives and if nothing else enough time for some quite reflection. He knew for sure that the way he had lead the firm till today would not work for taking the firm to the next level.

The following day began with the presentation of the course. The seminar room, laid out in a horseshoe pattern and with a gentle slope to guarantee all the participants a good view of the speakers, reminded him a little of the forums of ancient Greece, those agoras where the wise man exposed his knowledge to debate with his disciples, and where thought and discussion flowed. He sat in one of the back-row chairs, to one side of the seminar room; he still was skeptical about the real value-add he was going to derive from this seminar.

During the first three days the instructors of the various areas covered by the seminar spoke to the group. John took notes on the ideas that seemed important to him. And during the various breaks and rest periods he went over his notes and the material from the classes, wondering how he could tie all those ideas together and to what extent he could put them into practice in his enterprise. He also got involved in interesting debates with other executives.

The last day of the seminar was going to focus on the culture of innovation, the topic John was most interested in. Mike, the instructor, managed to get John's attention at the outset when he projected an image showing a gorilla, a chimpanzee and a monkey. And he made a curious analogy:

> "We could classify organizations by using this animal analogy. Gorillas are strong, have an impressive musculature and powerful teeth. They are respected by other simians. But they are slow, heavy and 'traditional'. They base themselves on the known and do little exploration, since they're sedentary. For their part, chimpanzees are more agile than the gorillas, and they explore their surroundings more, but only when moved by necessity. However, they are much more cerebral than the gorillas. By contrast, monkeys are in constant motion, they live in communities, they help each other, and they are constantly exploring new territories to be able to survive."

With quick strokes, Mike used several sheets of his flip chart to draw some diagrams showing the relationships between these animals and three different classifications of company types.

"So we'd have the large corporations, which we would relate to the gorillas, since they typically have muscle but not agility; the medium-sized companies, which would be similar to the chimpanzees, which are at an intermediate point—sometimes they lack muscle, and at other times, agility; and finally, we would have the small companies that would be like the monkeys, which have the least muscle and the greatest agility."

"And what am I referring to when I speak of muscle and agility in companies?" He moved away from the diagrams and looked at them as if trying to find the answer to his own question. He turned back to his audience. "Perhaps we could compare these traits to their ability to innovate, change their habits, their locations and their size."

Mike paused deliberately and observed the participants. They were expectant; some were taking notes, striving not to lose the thread of what he was explaining.

"In the same way, in the case of the simians we've used," he continued, "we see that the monkeys innovate: they generate change and take calculated risks of necessity, for example when they exhaust the food supply in the nearby bushes. To them, innovation is a means to an end. It's survival."

Mike underlined these last words under the drawing of the innovating monkeys.

Mike continued, "An end," he repeated to himself. "'action → reaction'. That is, 'I'm running out of food → I innovate'. Not bad...for monkeys. Getting back to the realm of the company, I would encourage you to conceive innovation not as an end, but as a journey. As the consequence of what we have the intention and purpose to be–and he gave full emphasis to the verb *be*–innovators. And to accomplish that we have to have a style, some skills and certain habits. Which is to say, a culture of innovation. And if we acquire those things, we won't find ourselves forced to innovate and take risks when our forage is exhausted and there's no other way out. Rather, for us this will be a standard practice for living that will ensure that we never lack food."

John watched Mike with skeptical curiosity. He was trying to evaluate what it was in Mike's first half-hour presentation that gave him this sense of unease. And he was unable to distinguish whether it was the discourse itself, the crushing obviousness of the message he'd just heard, or Mike's unconventional way of moving about in the seminar room, with several flip chart sheets filled with something that attempted to look like monkeys and gorillas spread around the room, instead of using the habitual antiseptic, well ordered computer projection. Or perhaps it was all of these things together.

The next half hour of the session seemed to change John's view a little. But, only a little. Mike presented a lot of data to show that firms in general were struggling with their innovation efforts. While senior executives all unanimously agreed that innovation was an important driver of growth, only a few managed it well. Most executives were disheartened with their innovation investments and programs and a lot were skeptical as to what it could actually deliver for the firm. So, Mike threw out quite a controversial question, "If firms around the globe are struggling, then do we even know what *innovation* is? Do we really understand this thing that we call *innovation*?" This question got several perplexed and confused looks from the audience.

Mike started out by saying, "I don't care what you have read about innovation, what other faculty have told you what innovation is and what your consultants have told you. I want to know what you think innovation is. I want to know what it represents for you personally." Mike went around the room asking each one of the two dozen executives to define what innovation meant for them personally in one sentence. As each person gave their version of what innovation was he kept recording on two flip charts one "key word" from each of their responses. John had not even realized what Mike had done and he was sure that unbeknownst to most participants Mike had recorded some responses in blue and some in green. All the blue responses were on the left flip chart and all the green ones were on the right.

Technology	**Opportunity**
R&D	**Risk**
Products	**Change**
Processes	**Disruptive**
New Markets	**Creativity**
Value	**Unique**
Solutions	**Breaking Rules**
Improvement	**Vision**
Evolution	**Paradigm Change**
Differentiation	**Experimentation**
Solving Problems	**Creating Needs**

At the end of this exercise, he turned around and asked the audience to summarize the group's views or thoughts about innovation. At this moment several people in the audience started seeing patterns. Their responses to the two categories were: cause and effect, inputs and outputs, enterprise vs. market, internal vs. external to the firm, and tangible and intangible. There were some funny and creative responses like light vs. dark and us vs. them and others. But Mike kept pushing them to think of different ways of expressing the two lists. He repeatedly kept asking them to think simple. Finally someone in the audience pointed out that the two big buckets or boxes were in fact left and right-brain activities. Mike continued:

> "We conventionally attribute (not scientifically) the left brain to be related to logic, cause and effect, linear, language, and structure. The right brain is associated with creativity, artistry, emotion, passion, peripheral vision, and holistic thinking. The first thing that we need to acknowledge is that Innovation is about the *whole brain*. The right brain plays an inordinately significant role in Innovation."[9]

He then went on to question the audience as to what was the last major investment or change effort that they, the audience, had undertaken in their own firms. The responses were quite predictable. Several of them had implemented or were in the process of implementing either a 6-sigma or some form of TQM initiatives. Some of them had put in ERP systems or were in the process of standardizing onto one system after being acquired or having made acquisitions. Other responses included CRM, ISO and re-orgs. He asked the group as to where the emphasis of these initiatives was. Was it left brain focused or right brain focused? There was resounding agreement that all these initiatives were very left brain focused.

Then Mike went on to remind the class of executives that in fact in our entire lives we have focused on training the left brain. The last major management discipline that was to sweep all businesses—TQM and 6-sigma—were very left brain oriented – highly structured, step-by-step scientific processes. So was the entire IT revolution, ERP and Supply Chain coordination and for that matter all of our MBA training and not to mention

---

[9] The traditional Right-Brain Left-Brain theory grew out of the work of Roger Sperry, who was awarded the Nobel Prize in 1981. More recent research shows that the brain is not nearly as dichotomous. However, we use the older model as a convenient way of organizing our thoughts to convey a point in a more familiar way.

our schooling. The current discomfort and disillusionment that executives are having with innovation is because they are treating it like every other discipline—left brain oriented—that came before it and it is not working. The results have been dismal in spite of putting a lot of resources and processes.

When Mike asked the group as to which of the two flip charts they were more comfortable with, the responses were again overwhelmingly obvious. He went on to say, that our understanding of innovation is where our understanding of quality was 20 years ago. We have just started to tap into our right brain and trying to understand how to manage it. Just as he was stopping for the coffee break he said, "The only thing that we as executives can do, is to create a climate where our people can be naturally creative. That's it." As everyone started to get up, he went to the board and drew:

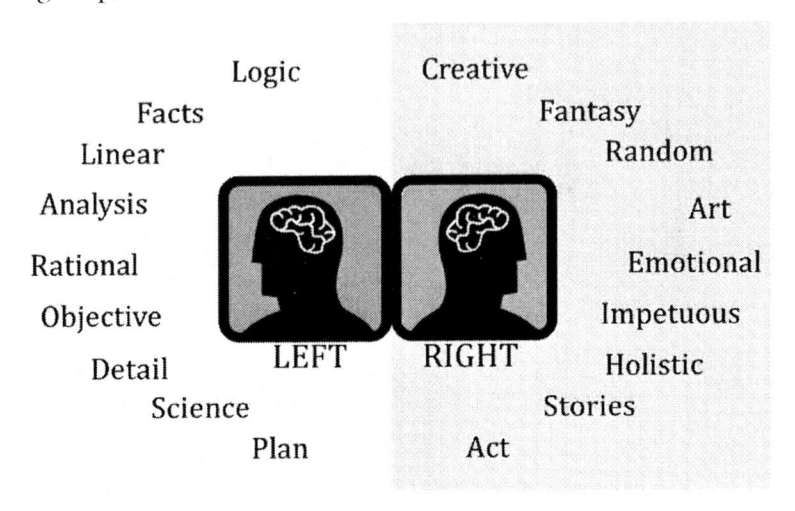

LEFT	RIGHT
Logic	Creative
Facts	Fantasy
Linear	Random
Analysis	Art
Rational	Emotional
Objective	Impetuous
Detail	Holistic
Science	Stories
Plan	Act

For John, this discussion was too simplistic. During the first coffee break, John accosted Mike with the intention of drawing some clarity out of the unease he felt.

"Hi, Mike. My name is John, and I'd like to tell you that I found your presentation really interesting. Although, if it's all right with you, there are a couple of ideas that disturb me—"

"Go ahead, John," Mike cut him off good naturedly. "What are those rebellious ideas of yours?"

"It's about your theories of the size of companies and their innovative capacities. What do you think would happen if a big company divided itself into small units and gave those units the agility typical of small companies? You'd have the gorilla's muscle and the monkey's agility—"

"Good thinking, John! You would unquestionably increase your probabilities of success," he said. "It would be an innovative company. And there are examples of that. But the companies that are organized from that standpoint are few, so today most organizations can still be segmented into those three blocks that I set out. What's more," Mike added, raising his index finger, "we often witness firms going the opposite way, for instance when a big company buys a small or medium-sized one that stands out because of its innovative qualities and, not long after it's been swallowed by the giant, the smaller company loses most of its innovative capacity, which is diluted in the whole and disappears. So, if the objective for the large corporation was to acquire an innovative culture, it has just failed. In most instances, the gorilla gobbles up the monkey and converts it into a mini-gorilla," Mike declared.

"That means there's still space for innovative companies that fill gaps or create new market niches" John declared.

"Of course!" said Mike in an emphatic, almost impassioned tone. "The world remains to be built. The manager or entrepreneur who thinks that everything's been done is dead! The future is full of opportunities that we aren't yet aware of. Think of many of the innovations that surprise us today, and that create new segments and markets: they didn't exist a few years ago—they couldn't even have been predicted."

Mike's energy awakened some of the participants' curiosity, and they approached to listen to the conversation.

"The fact is that human stupidity offers some of the best business opportunities," Mike concluded with a look of genuine amazement on his face.

"Well, if what you're saying is so obvious, how could we innovate more and better?" John asked.

Mike remained silent for a few moments, took a paper napkin from the coffee counter, wrote a sentence on it, folded it and handed it to John with a conspiratorial smile.

John unfolded the note as Mike continued, "All enterprises, whether they are startups or large, whether they are hierarchical, bureaucratic or flat, should first *desire* to be innovative; but above all, *disciplined* in their approach to innovation."

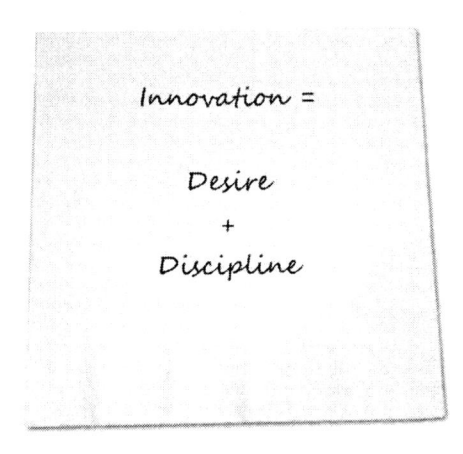

$$\text{Innovation} = \text{Desire} + \text{Discipline}$$

John was a little surprised with the choice of words—*desire* and *discipline*. Why those two words? He was fine with the first word. But what in the world did the second word have to do with a company's innovation? Old paradigms and referents came to him. He thought that there was nothing more disciplined than the army, and yet he didn't see it as a very innovative organization. He only thought that discipline would reduce initiative, increase conformity and kill creativity.

Meanwhile, Mike had diverted his attention to the participants who now surrounded them, with whom he'd started a discussion. John, with Mike's note in his hand, suddenly barged into the conversation without the slightest attention to good manners:

"Innovation and discipline?"

Mike focused again on John, as if he'd been waiting for him.

"John, quite often when we witness others' success we believe that innovation has more to do with a felicitous accident than with planned, constant and focused work. And it's not so. What's true is that discipline in innovation reduces the risk. And it's also true that entrepreneurial behaviors increase what may seem to be luck." Mike snapped his fingers in imitation of the Eureka response and made a disapproving face. "What is really unquestionable is that when we bring together entrepreneurial thought and disciplined action, we expose the organization to the dynamics of opportunity generation that, in time and with the consolidation of experience, makes the enterprise achieve a level of effectiveness that, to the outsider's eye, can only be seen as a stroke of luck."

"In my view mostly luck than reality," differed the contentious John.

"Mostly luck?" repeated Mike with a smile. "In my dictionary, luck is at the intersection of experience, hard work and creating opportunities. It is so with most experienced innovators as well"

John was still unconvinced, but in any case, took the paper napkin with Mike's note on it, turned it over and wrote:

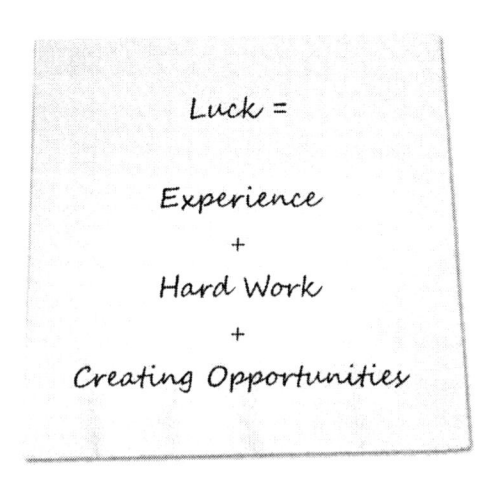

$$Luck = Experience + Hard\ Work + Creating\ Opportunities$$

And he showed it to Mike with the smile of a diligent student.

> "That's right," agreed Mike, shrugging his shoulders in a gesture of importance. "There are no shortcuts. Innovation, like culture is the outcome of our attitudes, actions, and behaviors. Moreover, it is a sequential process that is moderated by the firm's successes and failures and how the firm learns, reflects and metabolizes these experiences. Hence the DNA of an enterprise is a reflection of the people's DNAs."

Mike seemed to be convinced of people's innate creativity. It was clear that he believed in it wholeheartedly. Additionally, he seemed to be passionate in sharing his ideas. John—despite all his reluctance—seemed somewhat engaged by this instructor's discourse. Around them the group of curious participants was growing.

> "Innovation," Mike continued elaborating, "isn't a tool or panacea, but a consequence. It is the deliberate and intentional decision following an aspiration to want to be

innovative and this begs the question of creating a culture of innovation; and everything that such an effort entails."

"And we have to bear in mind that it's simple. We need only to seek out and manage something that's already inside of us. Adults need to be centered on pragmatism. This comes from us being constantly judging everything. That leads us to demand a nearly military discipline of ourselves when it comes to innovation. In childhood, however, we lived in a metaphysical world. Our world was one that was in constant search driven by curiosity. We were also much less judgmental and more accepting. Hence, it was eminently creative." Mike held a dreamy silence, as if he were revisiting his childhood for a moment.

"But this seems to contradict what you've just explained about discipline," John interjected.

Mike smiled and, bringing his index finger up to his lips, took the paper napkin that John had in his hand and said:

"You are focusing on the wrong word. Don't focus on the word innovation. The key word there is *desire*. Even as adults, when we are dealing with something that holds great interest for us, don't we persevere until we achieve it? For this reason, a good combination of desire and discipline is the key. Innovation is not a cause. It is an outcome."

John was listening, engrossed in Mike's explanations, when the professor realized it was time to return to the seminar room.

While he was returning to his seat, John felt a little less apprehensive. He was curious to know more, to continue the conversation he'd begun with Mike. His thoughts immediately turned towards his investment of time and money into this seminar and whether it was justified. He couldn't help smiling after thinking more about the last conversation. At most times for John this world seemed to be very binary—zeros and ones;

highly transactional—give and take; and instant gratification—easy answers. He was at the seminar thinking that spending a little time and money, he could learn quite a lot! However, John felt that for Mike it was not all rational and economic. He did not provide easy answers. He would ask difficult questions, make assertions and expect the audience to reflect.

John followed the rest of the session with a little more attention than before, just a little. He couldn't stop wondering…once the aspiration-discipline pair has been accepted as inseparable, what's the next step?

As the session got started, Mike was bombarded with questions. And as he went on addressing them one by one, John was again stuck by another assertion that Mike made: "Innovation is a Choice. And, so is survival." He followed this up with data to show the average age of a Fortune 500 firm, the average tenure of a Fortune 500 firm on the list and the relatively short lives of gorillas and even shorter lives of monkeys.

Just when John was going to ask, another participant also wanted clarification from Mike as to what he meant by "innovation is a choice." Mike went to the white board and drew a picture to show how firms can make choices about where they want to be in the future (see picture below). He went on to explain that it is entirely up to the executives to do nothing but to milk its current cash cows and end up at point C over a period of time. In fact, statistically, they wind up dead. On the other hand the firm could use the much prevalent quality techniques and continuous improvement methodologies to incessantly make small adjustments to their products, processes, markets, and business model to land at point B. Finally, a firm could opt to do a combination of continuous improvement and continuous experimentation to periodically come up with some quantum jumps in performance to be at point A. Mike termed these quantum improvements that happen as a result of continuous experimentation as "Radical Innovation" as against the continuous improvement philosophy that was akin to "Incremental Innovation." In other words, incremental innovations could be achieved by using many of the concepts and tools that were prevalent in lean and quality philosophies and quantum improvement is the fruit of continuous experimentation.

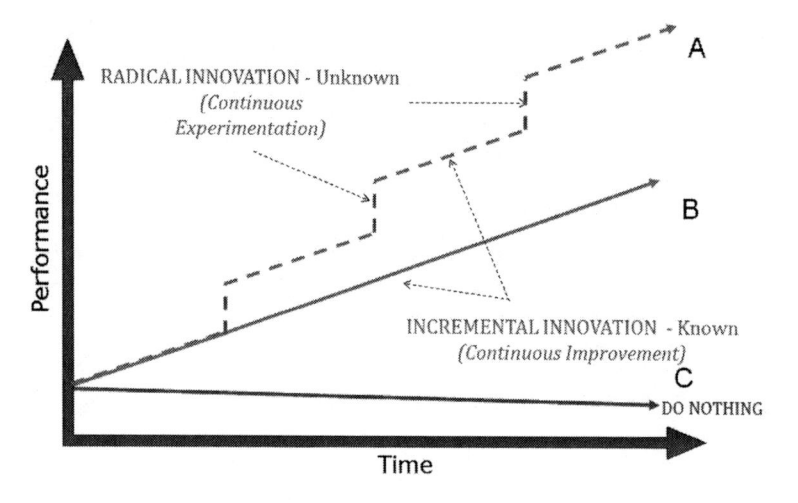

Chart: Performance vs Time showing three trajectories — A: RADICAL INNOVATION - Unknown (Continuous Experimentation); B: INCREMENTAL INNOVATION - Known (Continuous Improvement); C: DO NOTHING.

He further went on to explain some fundamental differences between the concepts of quality and innovation. While there are huge similarities in the approaches to incremental innovation and quality / six-sigma, there are also some fundamental differences. Quality is about reducing variance from a pre-determined standard while Innovation is about finding the variant and making it the standard. Quality is about eliminating exceptions while Innovation is about finding the exception. In Quality the process of reducing the variance by finding root causes of deviation is a highly structured, step-by-step, scientific method while the innovation process is about finding, shaping and capturing opportunities that involves significant amount of experimentation and failure. Quality is evolutionary while Innovation is revolutionary. Quality is about conformity.

Innovation is about freedom. Quality is about comparison, but innovation has no comparison. When there is comparison, there is competition. But, when there is no comparison, there is no competition. Hence, the capabilities that a firm needs in quality are quite different from the capabilities that it needs to develop in innovation.

INNOVATION = RADICAL + INCREMENTAL
&
INNOVATION IS A CHOICE

Most importantly, Mike made a distinction between the "known" world and the "unknown" world. He said that incremental innovation was based on known technologies, known products, known markets, known business models and known competitors. However, radical innovation was in the realm of the unknown—untested technologies, unknown markets, unfamiliar products, unproven business models and unidentified competitors. Hence the predictive strategies used for making incremental changes to the "known" world is vastly different from the emergent strategies used to uncover the "unknown" world. This discussion totally intrigued John.

During the lunch break, John tried to sit beside Mike in order to continue the conversation that had been interrupted. But luck would have it that Mike got tied up talking with other participants. So he would have to postpone assuaging his preoccupation, but he knew his mind was there, and he had no intention of giving it up. He'd find his opportunity to take up the subject again.

And his opportunity came in quite a simple way. After lunch, Mike came up to him in a cheerful mood.

> "John, you look as if you haven't stopped turning the subject of innovation over in your mind."

"To me it's a subject that's as fascinating as it is unknown," John admitted, using some of Mike's terms. But he continued, "I am still perplexed with your assertion about the role of discipline in innovation. Discipline for me means conformity."

"You are only partially correct. Yes, discipline for the most part is used to imply conformity, following rules and correction and punishment for deviating from the norm. I don't mean any of these when I refer to discipline in innovation," replied Mike.

"Then, what do you mean, Mike?"

"Well, that's for you to find out. I am using the word in its classical sense. I want you to go back to its roots to find out its true meaning. In fact I use the word discipline in at least four ways when it comes to innovation and none of them imply conformity and correction" said Mike.

"What do you say we meet this evening after class, and have a leisurely chat about it? We can walk into town—it's fifteen minutes away—where there's a coffee shop that has a very pleasant outdoor terrace bar. Let's see if you can transmit some of your passion to me!" Mike bantered.

"Sure, Mike, it'll be a pleasure!" John replied, quite surprised.

Chapter 3

The Discipline of Innovation

John and Mike set out on their stroll to the nearby town center. Because Mike, who lived in the area, knew the surroundings well, he steered them away from the main road, and they took a road that passed through a stand of elms that spread out behind the apartment building. It was a cool, bright spring day, and they welcomed the walk after so many hours shut away in the seminar room dealing with concepts and debates.

"Well," said Mike after they'd had a brief exchange of courtesies, "to me you look very anxious, and that's typical of youth or of people whose minds are laden with lots of thoughts. It's clear that both you and I are already in the latter group," and he let out a guffaw.

John couldn't help wondering what he was doing traipsing through an unknown wood with this talkative and somewhat learned man—for a moment the image of an imp crossed his mind. And because he was a man who had no penchant for fantasies and prima donnas, he felt his skepticism surface and create a survival moat barricading him. For John, innovation had to be creative but, in Mike's words, it also required discipline and perseverance, which were serious and restrained.

> "To put your mind at ease, I should add," Mike continued, unaware of John's thoughts, "that anxiety also characterizes a lot of innovators! But perseverance and grit is much more important than anxiety."

> "For example," Mike continued while pushing aside some low branches, "look at the world high jump record. At the turn of the century and early 1900s high jumpers used a technique called the scissors. But they had a hard time breaking the 2.0 meter barrier. Until somebody came along who thought something like this: 'And why don't we try doing it differently?' And that somebody started turning ideas over in his head and sharing his concerns with other people, until they hit on the idea of jumping over the bar by placing the entire body, at a given moment, in a horizontal position parallel to the bar. And that's what they did."

Mike stopped short and kept silent for a long time while he questioned John with his restless gaze.

> "Surely"—Mike spread his hands apart and lifted them to the height of his head as he raised the tone of his voice, showing his excitement—"the other competitors saw the pioneers as 'nuts' who would end up cracking their skulls open. But those pioneers with their innovative technique succeeded in raising the bar quite significantly—not centimeter by centimeter, but by a good handful of centimeters, i.e., a quantum leap. Not long after that, those who had forecast disaster were imitating the new technique!" He paused, lowered his voice and slowed his

speech down. "And with that, the record went back to rising gradually: centimeter by centimeter."

Mike fell silent and resumed walking. John followed him without speaking. After a full day with Mike in the seminar room he had realized that Mike enjoyed his own stories.

> "And so they continued, improving centimeter by centimeter until some 'other nuts' disrupted high jumping again by inventing a modification of the style that consisted of propelling the body over the bar, not with the body stretched out, but in a sequence in which a leg and an arm went over the bar first, followed immediately by the trunk and finally by the other arm and leg. They called it the straddle jump. And once again the record jumped a good number of centimeters. And suddenly those 'nuts' were new pioneers and…"

> "And everybody imitated them!" John interrupted him in complicity, despite his reticence.

> "Right!" said Mike. "And what do you think happened then?"

> "The record went back to its gradual ascent, improving centimeter by centimeter."

> "Obviously. Now tell me…do you think athletes still use the straddle jump technique?" Mike asked.

> "No, you're right, today's high jumpers roll over the bar on their backs."

> "That's right. One fine day some other 'nuts' started experimenting again and applying concepts from physics. They saw that if they totally changed the way of running up to the bar, taking a curved path and making use of centrifugal forces, they could add those forces to the ones developed by speed and the upward thrust to jump even

higher. But there was a 'problem': the jumper fell backwards. That 'extravagant' point prevented this approach from being taken seriously by competitors until Dick Fosbury won the gold medal with this method in the Mexico City Olympics in 1968.

"Today," Mike went on, giving his voice the tone of the end of a fable, "that's the usual style. And it will go by the way side when the next 'nuts' think up an alternative way to jump over the bar. So you can see that the cycle is always the same: some…"

"…nuts shattered the preconceptions," interrupted John, amused at Mike's narrative display, "others were incredulous, the nuts achieved their purpose, so that the incredulous would convert to the new style and so on."

"That's it!" Mike confirmed emphatically. "Innovators are very typically observed with perplexity, but sometimes they succeed in creating market segments, or creating products or services that didn't exist until that moment."

He continued, "John, the current world record has not been broken in more than 25 years. Can you predict if we have reached the limits with the current technique or can you predict which next technique will break the current world record?"

For several minutes, Mike waited for a response from John. John's silence was sufficient proof for Mike to continue, "Radical innovation is about the Unknown! You cannot predict the unknown. The only way to reveal the unknown is through continuous experimentation and at the heart of experimentation is failure. Humans hate failure!"

They kept walking in silence. They could already see the first houses of the town. They could hear dogs barking and car motors in the distance, on the highway.

"But I don't see very clearly how to fit this story in with discipline, luck and everything you wrote for me this morning on the napkin," John wondered aloud.

"Very simple, my friend. Who, besides a high jumper or his coach, could have enough information and experience to be able to recognize the limiting elements of current methods?" Mike responded quite naturally. "And of course, as you can surely imagine, before going to the first track meet and officially presenting that new style, they had to endure countless setbacks and make many failed attempts until they made all of the pieces of the puzzle that was the new style work together. And doing all that meant that they had to apply a lot, or a tremendous amount, of discipline."

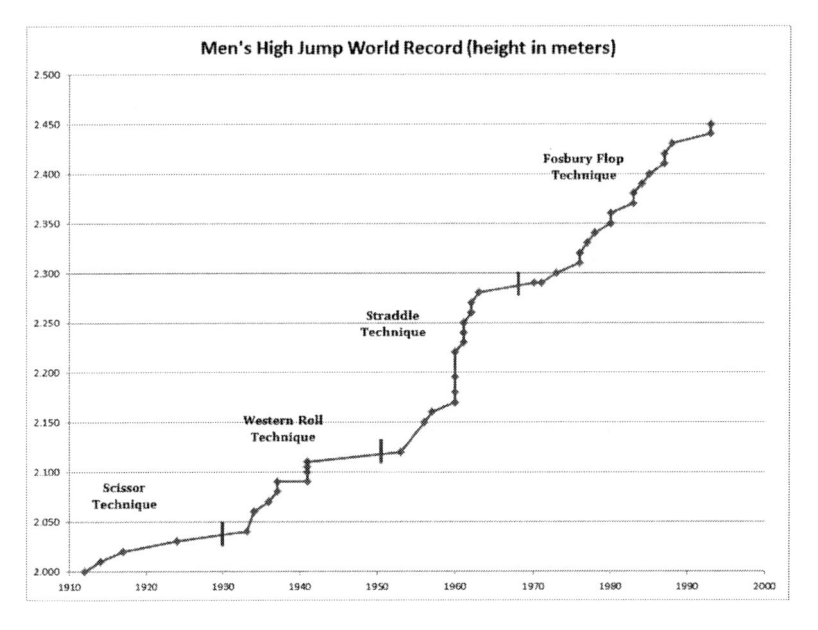

Men's High Jump World Record (height in meters)

- Scissor Technique
- Western Roll Technique
- Straddle Technique
- Fosbury Flop Technique

They arrived in the main part of the town, and in the central square was a café with tables on the street, several unoccupied. Mike indicated one of them and invited John to sit down.

"What'll you have? The coffee here is good, I recommend it to you. It's nothing like what they serve at the school!"

Mike entered the premises to order two cups of coffee, and came out again bearing a handful of paper napkins. He'd foreseen that they would be useful to them.

"I feel that I may be seeing the pieces a little clearer," said John before Mike could sit down. "But the pieces are still a little disjointed though. It takes a lot of courage to identify the fact that, by always doing things the same way, improvement is very linear, and that, on the contrary, if you question something to the hilt, you can make an improvement that amounts to a major leap forward. And surely those who achieved their objectives were described as having a lot of luck with the 'discovery'."

"That's the way it always is! And that's why, in my opinion, what many people call luck is nothing more than the result of an equation that, in general terms, could be: a lot of experience plus a lot of opportunity generation plus a lot of failures plus a lot of discipline and finally, a little bit of chance.

> Luck =
> Experience
> + Opportunity Generation
> + Failures
> + Discipline
> + Some Chance

John couldn't have agreed more with Mike's formula. Examples that fit into the equation immediately entered his mind: from the discovery of penicillin to the much more recent iPod. He also recalled that celebrated Edison saying that invention was 1% inspiration and 99% perspiration.

Mike savored his coffee and patiently allowed John to run through his thoughts. He imagined the whirlwind of ideas that must have been flowing through his head—his engrossed look gave him away.

"But then," doubting John took up the conversation again, "I don't think we should focus ourselves just on constant quantum jumps."

"No!" Mike cut him short drily. "Of course not! The market wouldn't accept it. People, and therefore the market, assimilate changes at a determined pace that we have to respect. The goal of all innovation is for it to make business sense, and that means that it must be able to produce a return, so that we can finance our next step. We have to measure our efforts, and not deviate for the sake of deviating."

"Remember, it is a choice" Mike continued, "companies must decide whether they want to pursue radical innovation or incremental innovation. Or both at the same time in certain proportion. While, incremental is necessary, it is not sufficient."

"Yes, I got that from this morning's session. My firm is pretty good; let me say we are very good at continuous improvement. In fact, we have mastered this in the last 4 or 5 years. But I clearly see the limits of just doing that," said John.

"What are those limits for your firm John?"

"Our products, processes, services, business model—everything that we do—are similar to what dozens of our competitors do. We copy each other quickly and all our products and services are highly commoditized. Not one firm in the industry stands out or can be called a clear innovation leader. Customer loyalty and entry barriers are ridiculously low."

"Sounds like a perfect time to break away from the crowd," said Mike, as he scribbled something else and slid the napkin towards John.

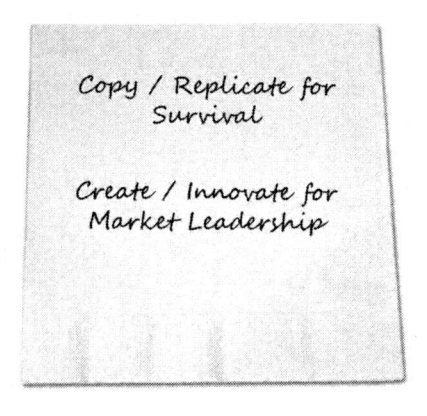

> Copy / Replicate for Survival
>
> Create / Innovate for Market Leadership

"John, there is absolutely nothing wrong with copying and replicating what competitors do. In fact, that is necessary for survival; but insufficient to thrive. I am glad to hear that you are very good at continuous improvement. Mastery at that will give you a huge advantage in mastering radical innovation and continuous experimentation."

"But Mike, you have not explained how do we become good at continuous experimentation? How do we become expert innovators? Where do we start?....... Err..., I don't know where to start?" John was sounding a little impatient.

Mike again seemed to have that smug look on his face; as though he was already expecting the question. This irritated John a little.

Mike again jotted something down on a napkin and pushed it towards John

"Thank you!" John smiled as he took the napkin Mike held out to him. And he added sardonically, "I'll keep it with the rest of my notes."

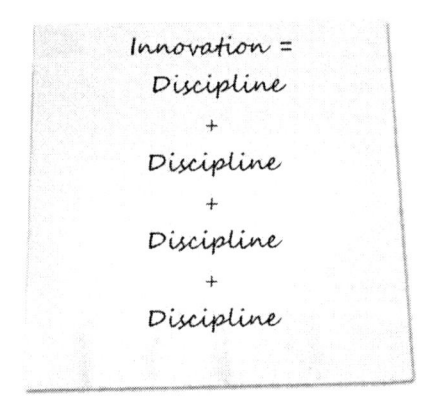

$$\text{Innovation} = \text{Discipline} + \text{Discipline} + \text{Discipline} + \text{Discipline}$$

At this point Mike's cell phone rang. He excused himself, got up and moved away to take the call. While Mike was absent, John tried to put his ideas in order. Not to put too fine a point on it, he had nothing more than a few napkins with a few laconic and very synthesized notes on them, which—although they might seem revealing—did not, in and of themselves, lead him anywhere. He still had some doubts as to whether Mike knew the answers to his concerns. But John also realized that Mike wasn't going to make it easy for him. Mike would make John travel the road and discover for himself some of the insights.

A few minutes later Mike was back. John then excused himself to visit the bathroom. And Mike took advantage of his absence to grab another napkin and jot down some more thoughts.

When John returned, Mike received him with the smile of a man who is comfortable with himself and his company. It was obvious that this man was having fun with the debate.

John, who had barely had time to sit down again, tossed out the question that had been resounding in his head for too long now.

> "What now, Mike? I think I understand one of the 'disciplines' but what about the other three?"

Mike leaned back in his chair in a very relaxed way and couldn't restrain a guffaw that started as controlled laughter but finally erupted into frank and open mirth.

John, patient but a little intimidated again, watched him. After a few moments, Mike regained his composure:

> "Pardon me, John, but during your absence, I thought about what your next question might be. Innovation is a discipline – a field of study – like 6-sigma, like Finance, like Biochemistry, like Law. It is like any other branch of knowledge."

Mike continued, "Every discipline has its own language. Each language has its own structure, its own principles, concepts and tools. When your firm learned the discipline of TQM and/or 6-sigma, they had to learn the basic concepts of lean thinking, process control, kanban, kaizen, etc. etc. In turn, each of these concepts had tools. Some had 7 tools others had 3 tools and some others had 9 tools."

> "Mike, I get it and we did cover some of this in class today!" said John. "But, do you mean to say that learning to innovate is like learning a new language?"

> "Ah! But there is a big difference in learning a language and mastering it. Take my Spanish for example. I have been exposed to it for more than 15 years now. But I can't say that my Spanish is any good. I can barely hold an intelligent conversation."

"Yes, I noticed that," John added with a big smile. "I heard you conversing with someone in the hallway this morning and you were struggling for words and your grammar was terrible. And, not to mention your verbs and your tenses."

"I know, I know! Don't rub it in John. I keep getting reminded of this at home" said Mike, in somewhat of an apologetic tone. But quickly threw another question back at John, "You speak several foreign languages. You said that your German is particularly good. How did that happen? Was it easy?"

"Oh! No! Not at all. It took me years to become proficient."

"Like all languages, most firms are able to learn the rudimentary aspects of innovation and some of its basic principles. But that doesn't mean that they are experts or masters at it," said Mike.

"Ah! Now I get the second discipline. You master a discipline through discipline," interjected John with a clear sense of satisfaction for having cracked one of Mike's codes.

"There you go John! But please remember what it takes to master any discipline. We went over these this afternoon."

"Yes, Mike. I recall; DESIRE, CHOICE, COMMITMENT, LINGUA FRANCA, CADRE OF EXPERTS, EDUCATE ALL EMPLOYEES THE BASICS, PERSEVERANCE & GRIT!"

"John!! That's good. Very good. Most people don't remember anything by the end of the 3-hour session. You are different."

"Mike, I have the DESIRE!"

"Bravo John! That is half the battle!"

Mike then somewhat eased back into the chair, as though he had reached a milestone in their marathon. For a while, the two of them just sat there enjoying the beautiful spring evening and the relaxed bustle of the small town center.

"You're right Mike, this coffee is good!"

Just as Mike was expecting, John posed the next question, "Mike, I am not so sure that we can be disciplined about innovation from day one. Firstly, I am still not very clear about the journey you mentioned in class today." And, Mike took out another napkin and started scribbling.

"Almost all learning follows this archetype,"[10] said Mike, pushing the napkin towards John.

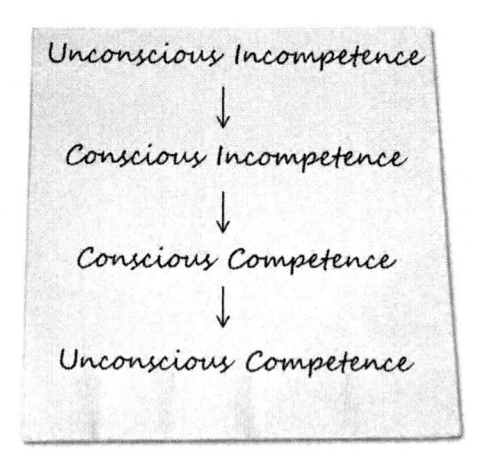

Unconscious Incompetence
↓
Conscious Incompetence
↓
Conscious Competence
↓
Unconscious Competence

John read the napkin and the message seemed familiar to him; he'd come across this sometime before, but he'd never paid much attention to it, let alone it being connected to innovation.

---

10. Learning Stages Model developed by Noel Burch at Gordon Training International over 30 years ago.

He reflected a bit, but couldn't manage to make the connection between the four stages of learning and innovation.

Seeing John a little perplexed, "Well, until now we've talked about the concepts of radical and incremental innovation, the difference between quality and innovation. We have talked about innovation as being a discipline as in a field of knowledge and about the need for two more disciplines—purposeful practice and grit or perseverance—to master it. These are all basic concepts to set the stage we want to walk across, but—and with this I'm going back to the core of it all—we can't forget that all companies that aim to be innovative need to have a culture of innovation. Do we agree up to this point?"

"Uh-huh," John corroborated.

"For an organization, a culture of innovation is not improvised from one day to the next; it's not something you acquire overnight."

"My friend John, if you want your enterprise to be innovative, you have no option but to undertake *The Journey* to create a culture of innovation. As an enterprise, we have to learn to become innovators. And this journey is like any other classic learning process. That's what I mean by an archetype—a universal principle. As you well know, almost all learning requires passing through these four stages, through which we've passed in all the learning experiences we've undertaken since our earliest childhood. We all start at the same point, I don't know what I don't know, i.e., unconscious incompetence. Firstly, we don't want to re-invent the wheel. So, we look at what others have already said and experienced, i.e., existing body of knowledge. We acquire this knowledge and realize that there is a lot more to be learnt, i.e., you reach the conscious incompetence stage. Then, we try to turn our knowledge into action; we know what we have to do and how to do it. Through purposeful practice, which is another form of discipline, we become consciously competent. However, expertise is only achieved by being courageous and determined, yet another form of discipline. When we are experts, we don't even think about it, i.e., unconscious competence. We just live it, breathe it and just do it."

Mike took up the napkin back from John to add something else.

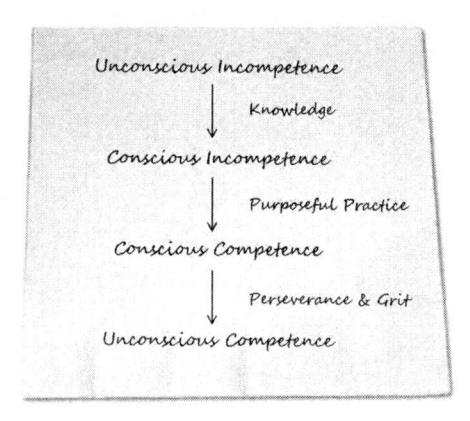

```
Unconscious Incompetence
         │ Knowledge
         ↓
Conscious Incompetence
         │ Purposeful Practice
         ↓
Conscious Competence
         │ Perseverance & Grit
         ↓
Unconscious Competence
```

John was nodding in agreement as he said, "Mike, you have a knack for taking people from clutter to clarity. I feel I am learning quite a bit through this dialog."

> "Thanks John. After all, that is my job. Isn't it? And, to your credit John, not all executives come into a dialog with a totally open mind. We will talk about 'the open mind' a little later."

Mike continued, "So, to finish up this concept, the first time our parents gave us a spoon and we plastered the baby food onto our cheek, because we weren't capable of finding the hole of our open mouth, the learning process to mastery has been the same. Once we had the process internalized, we've always done it without thinking about it. So, I call the three steps of

Learning as Knowledge → Purposeful Practice → Perseverance & Grit as 'Knowing,' 'Doing' and 'Being.' Only now we're adults and we know the mechanisms of learning very well. So, why should it be more complicated now?"

> John's skepticism seemed to be dissipating slowly as he spoke, "Mike, I want to buy you dinner so we can continue talking for a while longer."

Mike hesitated a little, but quickly made his decision, "Let me call home and tell them not to expect me for dinner. Since I travel so much, whenever I am in town I always try to have dinner with my family. But I am sure that they will excuse me for one evening."

> "I am sorry for being so selfish and for taking time away from your family."

> "Don't worry about it John, I wouldn't be sitting here if I was not having fun. Please remember, I am learning every time that I am interacting with an executive. Sorry to reduce you to a data point, but this is research for me." And they both laughed.

Chapter 4

The Practice and Dynamics of Innovation

John was beginning to discern where Mike was leading him. The analogy with our childhood learning experiences in fact clarified several things about how enterprises learn. He had already seen clearly during the day's session that in his teaching, Mike believed in applying the technique of stimulating his audience so that they would reach their own conclusions. He didn't stand on a pulpit and launch all the theory at once, but dosed it out so that his students would have time to metabolize a concept, generate their questions and move on to the next step. He also knew now that for Mike, innovation was a game, and he'd started to get into that game. Although he knew that this game was nothing more than cunning arguments wielded by an imp who was trying to pull those who had a few grams of entrepreneurial spirit out of their routine.

Night had fallen. The faint lights of the square created a very comfortable atmosphere. A couple of more tables were now occupied, and the rhythms of their neighbors' conversations drifted over to them. Passing cars were few and far between. John found it a good place to escape from the usual pressures that condition us; it was a good place for the spirit to lower its guard and for the mind to become clear and receptive.

He expressed his thoughts to Mike, and the professor's satisfied smile confirmed that he had long since reached the same conclusion.

> "That's the very reason I settled here several years ago. But don't delude yourself; I can be here, I have to be here, but your place is on the front line of the battle." He smiled his mischievous smile, raising his hands in a gesture of mock apology. "My job is simply to recharge your batteries, to broaden your horizons smothered by day-to-day pressures. It's people like you, the executives and entrepreneurs, who really make things change and move forward, who keep us alive."

They were silent for a while, as they enjoyed the peaceful surroundings, the darkened landscape with the woods silhouetted against the night sky. Then they talked for a while about their lives, their families, as two good friends would have done. They ordered dinner. Mike again placed some more napkins in the center of the table with the learning sequence.

> "The ball is in your court. You can now lead your enterprise on this journey towards a culture of innovation!"

> "Don't make fun of me. You know that I still have a long way to go before I can decipher your hieroglyphics, let alone lead my firm into this totally foreign territory. Well, I don't know, perhaps you'd carry my backpack for me, that would be great."

> "Let me see what I have digested so far." John picked up the written napkins and started thumbing through them

as though they were some sort of a map while Mike refilled both their wine glasses.

"Mike, please, give me some more clues about the three concepts that you've included among the steps of the learning sequence. What is this Knowledge step? How do you Practice? What is this purposeful practice? How can an enterprise get the Discipline, as in Grit and Perseverance?"

Mike laughed with gusto. He took the napkin out of John's hands and placed it in the center of the table again.

"Very simple, John. Let's step back again. If, as we've agreed, we see innovation not as a means, but as a consequence, it's because we create a culture where ideas are systematically and routinely converted into opportunities. Then there won't be a need to force the enterprise to innovate."

"John, humor me here for a minute. Just for a brief moment, let us step back in history, way way back. Why do you think the Cro-Magnons outnumbered, outlasted and eventually wiped out the Neanderthals, even though the Neanderthals' physiology was much better suited for the northern European cold and they had acclimatized there for a much longer time than the recent Cro-Magnon émigrés?"

"If I remember my history right, the Cro-Magnons were better organized and had better hunting tools."

"John, you are absolutely right! Why were they better organized and why did they have better hunting tools than the Neanderthals? How were they able to organize themselves in a better fashion and how did they come up with better hunting tools? "

"Ah! Now I remember, the Cro-Magnons had a much more evolved language as compared to the Neanderthals."

"Bingo John! You got it. Not only did they have better hunting tools, the Cro-Magnons had better tools in general that helped them to have better art, better clothes and better shelter against the cold. All these innovations were cultural and at the core of the cultural stimulus was language. A common language creates a community, strengthens a team, it enables the community members to defend themselves, develop, take care of each other and organize themselves."

"Humans are primarily engaged in three major activities during their waking hours; we are either learning, working or playing. We do all these three activities as a part of a community. All innovations happen in a community. But, there is a difference in the details. While more than 90% of all patents, i.e., inventions, are given to groups of 3 or less, almost all innovations, i.e., commercialization of these inventions, are done by communities. Haven't you ever wondered why the Nobel prizes are always awarded to mostly individuals and in some occasions shared among two or three people at most and in even rarer situations to an institution?"

"What you are saying is that inventions are more like individual sports but innovations are like a team sport" said John.

"John, I love that analogy. May I use it? Of course, I promise to attribute it to you." And they both laughed.

Mike continued, "A community is a group of interacting organisms, not just humans, sharing an environment. In humans, this also refers to a group that is organized around common values and social cohesion. At the core of any community is a common language. It is the fundamental basis for the existence of a community. A *lingua franca* is a language systematically used to communicate between persons not sharing a mother tongue. All disciplines—management, medicine, law—have a *lingua franca*. So does Innovation. The first step to create a community of innovators is to teach them the lingua franca of innovation – its principles, its frameworks, its concepts and tools."

> "Once they learn the lingua franca, they will be able communicate on the same wavelength, act and work together and practice what they have learnt together in the realm of innovation and perform at a very different level of effectiveness. Then they will start having their own habits and traditions. This will eventually lead to a culture of innovation." Mike kept nodding in agreement as John spoke rapidly. Almost like a kid trying to please the parents after having mastered a new trick.
>
> "Bravo, John!" exclaimed Mike, who was listening intently. "No lingua franca, no culture."

John was beginning to warm up and have some fun; it had been a long time since he had felt this unfettered.

Mike leaned back and smiled. "John, you should give yourself more credit than you normally do. You skipped a few details here and there, but you now have the general idea. Except that habits and traditions are built up over time. Remember when— 15 or 20 years ago—companies started to focus on quality; since that time those companies have created experts in Total Quality Management and 6-sigma within their organizations. Experts trained in the language of quality – principles, concepts and tools. They move around the enterprise in a cross-disciplinary fashion and cooperate with the departments or business units to improve quality and to reduce costs. Now we need to create the same conscious expertise in terms of innovation."

> *Start building a Community by giving them the lingua franca of innovation – its principles, concepts and tools.*

This time it was John who pulled out a napkin and he jotted down:

And Mike started laughing heartily, "John, I can almost picture you doing this with your executive team...... In fact, do you know that one learns best when one has to teach something to others?..... In any case, you are on the mark. The absolute starting point for the culture of innovation journey is to start creating a community by giving them the lingua franca of innovation – its principles, concepts and tools."

Still with a big grin on his face, Mike got up and went to the cashier's table. He brought back a bunch of crayons—the ones that kids are given in all restaurants—and a couple of sheets of paper. He sat down and began drawing some graphs and diagrams.

For a while, there they were, one engrossed in his thoughts and the other drawing colored lines and circles, when the waiter served their dinner. The young man observed them with amusement, and was careful to serve the dishes without disturbing them. Both turned and smiled at the waiter as he left the table.

The Discipline & Culture of Innovation

"After covering this first link in the learning chain," John continued, "Mike, now please help me with the *practice* link. How do you practice what you have learnt?

"Very simple: as in any facet of learning in life, we have to practice so that the concepts become anchored in our *modus operandi*, until they become almost mechanical habits. And the same thing must happen in innovation. Except that the risks we run if we don't practice enough, after investing all sorts of resources in the previous step—education—are waste, loss of motivation, impatience, pressure...and, what's worse, the absence of results. To avoid falling down that very dark well, we've got to be agile and get down to action right away. The simplest tactic to avoid falling into chronic procrastination is to apply it to real projects, following the slogan 'Catch a fish while you're learning to fish'."

"So John, in reality learning and practice is not really sequential. They are and should be simultaneous. At the heart of practice is the process of going from ideas to opportunities and it looks somewhat like this...." Mike sat up at the table with the paper he'd been coloring and drawing on a while ago and pushed the sheet towards of John:

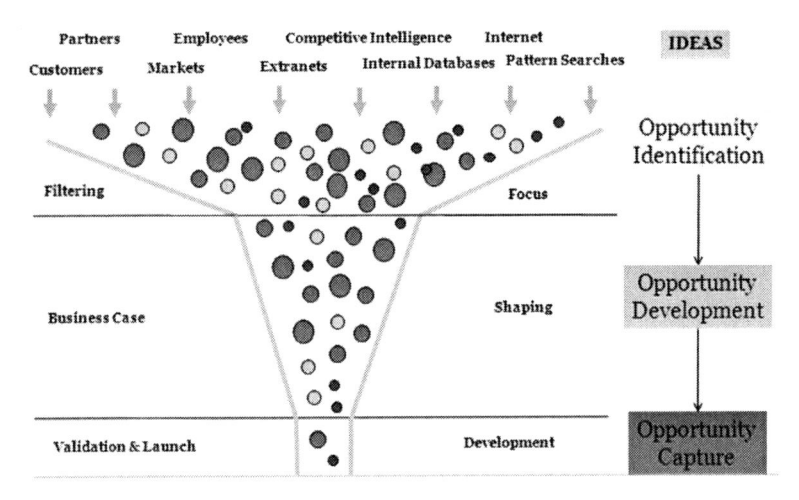

"While we are working on our lingua franca, we can actually get going with Innovation in Action, which is a systematic process of three actions that will enable us to advance from ideas to opportunities: generation, selection and development. Phase one: free generation and filtering of ideas, the more the better, always bearing in mind the focus where we want to generate innovation. Phase two: specification of the opportunities that have passed the first filter; we'll have to dig deeper into them to verify which ones hold up and show signs of being able to bear fruit. Phase three: we give the green light to the opportunities that have passed the selection process; the only remaining step is to prioritize them according to our resources and needs and set them in motion."

"That makes sense," John murmured to himself.

"Yes, it does, but it also harbors a lot of traps which, if you don't take them into account, can cause all the effort and systematizing not to give us the desired result," Mike emphasized.

"We have to involve in the idea generation process all the agents who are capable of contributing, describing their hopes, their fantasies, their interests.... whatever their hierarchical rank or relationship with the organization may be. That's why it's very important to listen to your suppliers, customers, and even to observe your competitors. There are several barriers here. Ideas are lost as a result of people's not expressing them explicitly because they believe it's not worth the effort to do so, or because they're expressed and then lost in the hierarchy or in some department that acts as the organization's black hole. So we need mechanisms so all of those agents can express their ideas, and there must be some 'automatic mechanisms' that facilitate the exploration of those ideas to convert them into opportunities that can go into the selection funnel."

Mike reached out and took another napkin to scribble.

John saw the note and looked a little puzzled as he said, "Mike, help me with this one. I am not sure I get it."

> *Ideas*
>
> *are*
>
> *not*
>
> *Opportunities!*

"John there is a caveat, it is painful and expensive to sift through ideas. As a matter of fact, I don't even like the word *ideas*. Firstly, the media, a multitude of idiot-savant blogs and even some well-known consultants and academics have added to this confusion by popularizing the term 'ideas.' In most situations, ideas are low-hanging-fruit that the firm should have implemented already in order to stay in business or stay-abreast with industry-standards. On the other hand opportunities add to the top line growth and/or profitability, by going into new markets, creating new products/services, building new capabilities and/or changing business models. So, you need to help people understand the difference between ideas and opportunities."

"In short, ideas are opinions........John, did you see any of the Dirty Harry movies?"

> "I loved Dirty Harry." John leapt forward stealing Mike's words from his mouth, "Opinions are like assholes, everybody has one, and they all stink. Dead Pool 1988."

Both of them start laughing loudly and Mike was clapping as he almost lets out a scream. All of this had attracted attention—furtive glances and looks of annoyance—from the other tables. Mike quickly regained his composure.

> "When I work with firms, executives often complain to me that their people do not have good ideas. On the other hand, I also hear employees at all levels complain that their bosses don't listen to their ideas. John, have you noticed that in your firm?"

A serious look suddenly came across John's face as he reluctantly nodded in agreement. He was recalling the improvised way in which he had tried to get his management to build ideas for change and was secretly ashamed of this failed attempt.

Mike continued,

> "Opportunities are ideas that will potentially generate growth in arenas that the firm intends to operate in the future. Most executives do not articulate this opportunity space well for their people. Very often, people may come up with great ideas, but they may not be opportunities for that specific firm. So, a better understanding among the people about the rough arenas the firm wants to play in and the approximate vehicles they want to use to get there will greatly increase the quality of opportunities that should flood the funnel."

> "Mike, I understand the distinction. Forget opportunities for the moment, in general our people are reluctant to voice their opinions, even if we try to solicit them explicitly. Even if they contribute, they seem to be all over the place."

"You are absolutely right John. Don't expect that your funnel will fill magically. Please remember that they do not have the language, the concepts and the tools. What most firms experience is garbage in / garbage out."

"Yes, you are right."

"Don't expect the funnel to fill up and be meaningful till you have educated a significant portion of the workforce; at least at a rudimentary level. Also, you shouldn't expect each individual to become an expert in this area. Just awareness can in fact significantly raise the overall performance of the community."

"Again John, there is a common mistake that a lot of firms make. When starting the journey, several executives do not learn the essentials of innovation—either due to lack of time or lack of interest. This can cause harm at a later stage since they do not have the same *lingua franca* as people who are working around them or they are in decision making capacities for approval of opportunities. Firstly, they won't know all the vicissitudes that innovation always entails. Secondly, this ignorance might cause them to either not appreciate or even outright block/condemn some of the practices and behaviors of those who are trying to pursue certain opportunities. This directly leads to at least three major problems: (1) good opportunities could be lost (2) people feel deflated that their leaders are not walking the talk and (3) good people may in fact leave the firm to pursue some of the identified opportunities by themselves. In summary, you don't want ignorant executives to be flow stoppers in your funnel."

"Mike, I want to go back to the nature of opportunities. I have somewhat tried this before. My executives are smart and they are eager to share their opportunity analysis with the team. But, when it comes to taking ownership and driving a specific opportunity, there seem to be few people stepping up to the plate; in fact no one steps up."

Mike mumbled "Again, no surprises here;" with a small smirk. He continued, "There are at least two major reasons for that. The first one is fairly easy. Your best and brightest are usually running your highest volume generator or mature cash-cows, aren't they?" And he paused.

After pondering for a while, John replied, "Come to think of it, you are right. Most of them but for a couple."

"I am sure their plates are full and they are usually fire-fighting everyday stuff. They just don't have the time or the bandwidth to take on extra projects. Am I right?" questioned Mike.

"Yep," nodded John.

"The second reason is fear," Mike pulled out another napkin and scribbled:

> *It is a failure fraught funnel.*

"By its very nature, most innovation projects fail. Most executives are scared of failure. In fact, they get to become executives primarily because of a string of successes. And, in most firms, in the wake of every failed project are fired people. So, executives want to work on projects with low uncertainty, let alone ambiguity."

"Mike, I lost you on the last sentence. What is the difference between uncertainty and ambiguity?"

Mike scribbled another note and said "All opportunities have at least one of three characteristics.

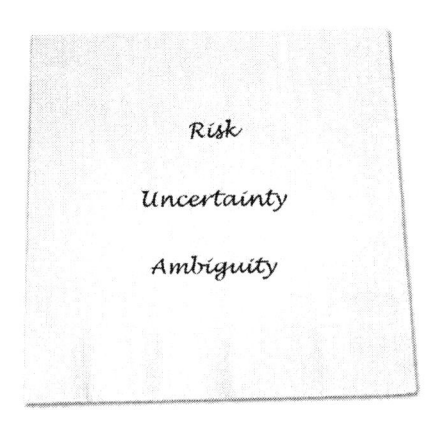

Risk

Uncertainty

Ambiguity

"Opportunities that deal with your existing business capabilities and exiting markets are usually derivative projects. A good example would be introducing an updated version of already existing software. Here you are dealing with known variables. The processes and outcomes are well known but may have some known risks associated with them. One can reasonably estimate those probabilities based on the firm's prior experiences and past data using analytical techniques."

"Opportunities that are more complicated have uncertainties. Uncertainty is about 'known unknowns.' Here the variables are generally known, but their distributions may not be fully clear. Examples would include creating a completely new platform from scratch to serve existing customers or trying to reach a very different customer base with your existing business platforms. Here you are stretching into adjacencies either the capabilities of the business model or the customer set the firm is serving."

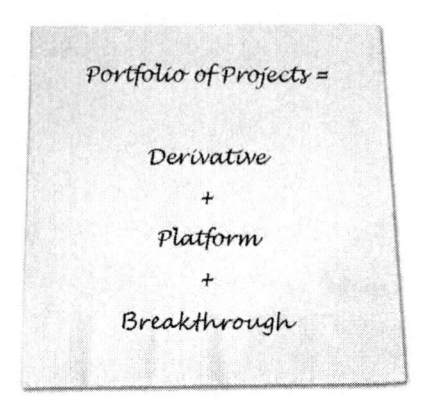

> Portfolio of Projects =
>
> Derivative
> +
> Platform
> +
> Breakthrough

"On the other hand, ambiguity lies at the heart of complex opportunities. Ambiguity is about 'unknown unknowns.' In these situations there is no clarity as to what variables exist in the decision space. Here, the firm has no previous experience exploring such opportunities and hence it is a significant leap for the firm that results in a breakthrough. Here the firm may be exploring entirely new technologies or new business models or creating new customer needs that other firms have not tried before." Mike reached out and pulled another sheet of paper.

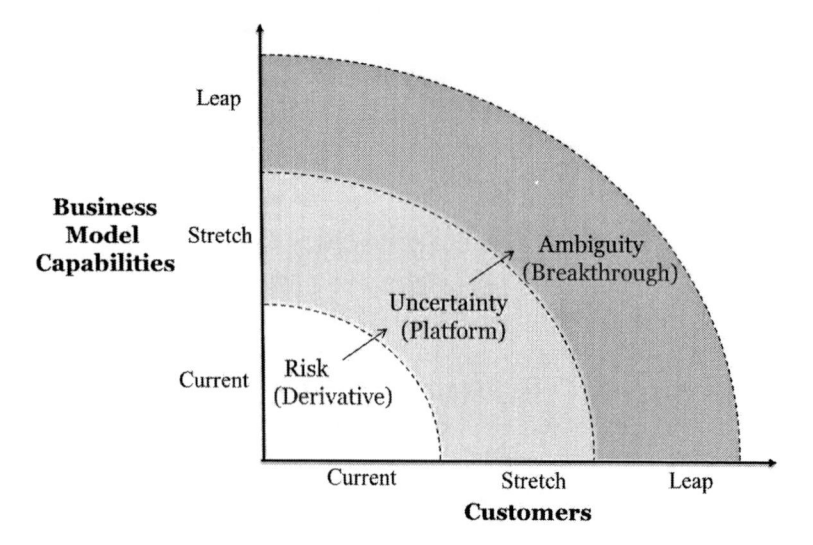

John took the paper in hand and stretched out his leg on the side of the table. He was quite overwhelmed with the multitude of concepts that Mike had introduced in such quick succession. Several minutes passed as Mike let John mull over the sheet of paper. John slowly raised his head and commented, "We do the derivative projects very well. But, as far as I can recall, we have barely even ventured into platform type opportunities; perhaps only twice in the last 10 years. And, we are all fully aware of the limits of just doing derivative projects."

And the silence continued for a while longer, till John again seemed to somewhat apologetically say, "Doesn't say much about my team or our capabilities huh?"

> "John, don't be too hard on yourself or your team. Incremental-ism is not unique to your firm. It is rampant among most medium and large firms. Radical innovation will not happen unless your executives learn to fail. That is the only thing that I can promise you about innovation."

John went pensive again and Mike was giving him the space to reflect. After all, learning to fail was at the heart of leading change and eventually the road that John will have to pave on their journey to create a culture of innovation.

After several minutes John broke the ice, "how can I help our executives learn to fail?"

> "Again John, Bravo! You are asking the right question."

Mike continued. "You need to do two things. One, the projects that they choose to work on during their practice will become all important. Then, you need to provide a safe and controlled environment while they practice; as they slowly venture into platform and breakthrough opportunities. You need to provide that safe sandbox where they can play and learn. If all projects succeed, probably they are not stretching themselves. Everyone will feel good, but they will not learn to fail. At the same time, if all the assigned projects fail, that will demoralize the team even if there are no repercussions."

John took his time to ruminate and respond, "And if this is the way it works—and I have no doubt that it is—all you need to do is tell me what is the purpose of repeating *discipline* at this point."

Amused, Mike applauded.

"Well, John, now I can go home and you can go back and convert your enterprise into an innovation machine."

"Mike, don't toy with me. I am very vulnerable right now. It's not often that all my weaknesses are exposed and that too in such a short time."

"Wonderful John! It takes a gutsy person to admit that. We all learn better when we are open and vulnerable. If you or I have all the answers then our conversation would suck! As I mentioned before, a good leader is measured on the quality of the questions, not their answers. A point that is often lost among most executives."

"Mike, I know I am still a little cloudy about this culture stuff. A few elements still seem to be missing and I have a weird feeling that *discipline* has something to do with it."

"You are right again," replied Mike as he looked at his watch. But then, he reached out to the bottle to pour out the remaining wine into their glasses.

Chapter 5

The Culture of Innovation

It was now completely dark; they had practically lost track of time. John was beginning to feel a bit tired, and was wondering how they'd get back to the residence building, but he didn't want to ask Mike for fear of straying off the subject. He could see the process and practice quite clearly. He was also very comfortable about the notion that repeated practice leads to discipline. But he wanted Mike to clarify this progression from 'Knowing' to 'Doing' to 'Being'."

He again gently prodded, "Mike, please help me to cross this bridge from 'Doing' to 'Being'. How can I move my firm from Conscious Competence to Unconscious Competence?"

> "John, most start-ups and small firms, usually gain a foothold in the industry by innovating once. All they need to do is find one opportunity in the market place in order to enter and thrive. Unfortunately, for established firms and for mature firms to survive and grow, you have to find opportunities routinely; repeatedly. You cannot

innovate once and hope that your firm will reap its benefits forever. That is where discipline comes in handy." He pulled out another napkin and scribbled.

"Please remember the overall goal is still to create a culture of innovation and culture is an outcome, a consequence."

"Mike, what do you mean it is a consequence?"

"John, to understand this, remember that we went through this in the class today. We discussed how other management disciplines evolved over time. In particular, we talked about the evolution of the field of 'quality'."

"Yes. Yes, Mike, I recall that. It is quite clear that this practical, comprehensive approach helped the critical principles and practice of quality to percolate into a majority of the firms world-wide," replied John.

"Most importantly, quality became a disciplined—deliberate and determined—activity with a great degree of predictability," replied Mike.

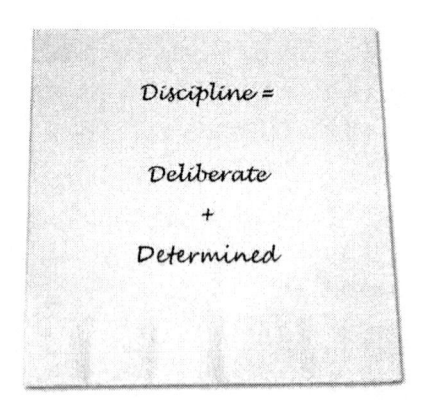

Discipline =

Deliberate
+
Determined

"*Deliberate* is about being purposeful and systematic. Deliberate is purposeful practice. Purposeful practice is intentional with a specific outcome in mind. Purposeful practice has intermediate goals, focused coaching, structured support systems and measured feedback. Systematic is about being organized, comprehensive, rigorous and thorough. Finally, *Determined* is about resolve and perseverance. In other words it is about courage and grit" asserted Mike.

Mike quickly added, "Similarly, building a Culture of Innovation is also an intentional, systematically planned and organized activity with a certain degree of predictability."

"Mike, if this is so logical, why isn't Innovation more widely implemented? Why isn't its practice more prevalent?"

Mike was again nodding his head as he complimented John, "very good question John."

"There are several reasons for this and we have touched upon some of these already. Firstly, our understanding of innovation is where our understanding of quality was 20 years ago. Interest in innovation, research and courses in innovation exploded only in the last 20 years. It was primarily fueled by the rise of the dot-coms that threatened the viability of traditional business models in several industries – music, media, telephony, retailing, reservations, financial services etc. So, most executives who are running large businesses today never had a course in innovation during their MBA programs. So, some of them are skeptical, others are scared and a few couldn't care less."

"John, do you remember Lewis Carroll's story, Alice in Wonderland?"

"Yes, I do. But, what about it?"

> "There's a point where Alice feels terribly lost in the nether world and while she is wandering she comes to a fork in the road. On the branch of a tree nearby she sees a Cheshire Cat, and the cat is laughing about the fact that Alice is lost. Alice then turns to cat and asks: Would you tell me, please, which way I ought to go from here?"

The Cheshire Cat replies, "That depends a good deal on where you want to get to."

So Alice replies, "I don't much care where…"

Then the cat replies, "Then it doesn't matter which way you go."

Then, Alice thinks for a moment and adds: "…so long as I get somewhere."

Then the cat says, "Oh, you're sure to do that, if you only walk long enough."

Mike fell silent. The silence made itself felt; almost all the tables in the restaurant were now empty. John listened with pleasure to his new friend, who never failed to surprise him with his inexhaustible repertoire of stories. After some long minutes in silence, Mike spoke again.

> "John, there are two words I like in this conversation. Alice is 'longing' to get somewhere. That is desire. There is hunger and thirst. And the second long is that, it is a 'long' journey." As he finished the sentence he picked up another napkin.

> "Mike, you mentioned this before; about desire and discipline," John said, as he read the napkin.

> Innovation =
>
> LONG
>
> +
>
> LONG

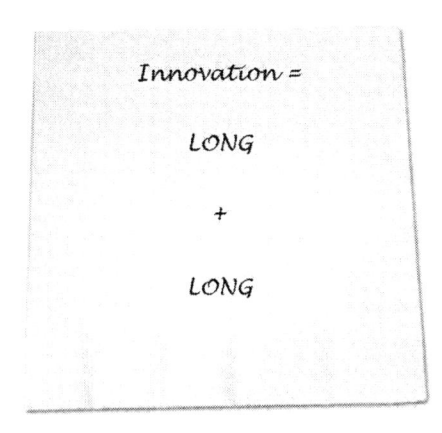

"Yes John, if you don't long to be innovative don't start the journey. It is the longing—desire and hunger—that will keep you disciplined—determined and resolute—to pursue the long journey. As you know most executive teams neither have the desire nor the wherewithal for this tedious journey. Organic growth is hard work, it is much easier to just buy growth. It is much easier to buy innovation than to create a culture of innovation."

"But Mike, I disagree; these same executives do seem to invest in long and tedious projects like 6-sigma, ERP implementation, post-merger integration activities and the like. So, how do you account for that?"

"Good point John. Do you recall one of the first things that we discussed in class today about innovation and how it is different from other management disciplines that have preceded it?"

"Ah! Yes, Mike. Sorry, I think I am getting a little tired. Not to forget the overwhelming amount of information that I have tried to absorb today." He paused.

Mike intervened to help John out, "Let us pick up on the fact that innovation has a huge right brain component that most of the preceding management philosophies and disciplines did not have. Also, please remember that all these disciplines evolved and gained popularity in the last century when we lived for nearly 100 years under Taylor's scientific management methods and the very rational approach to human productivity. These same principles and methods were applied to motivation as well; without much thought."

> "Yes Mike, but specifically, wasn't this carrot-and-stick motivational technique that gave rise to the productivity boom in manufacturing?"

> "Oh! Absolutely. It still works very well when the technologies are known, the products are known, the customers are known and the processes and the outcomes are well known. But, today most of those motivational techniques have been discredited; especially when it comes to creativity and innovation. In the knowledge world, and innovation is a knowledge based discipline, our traditional carrot-and-stick methods are completely obsolete. Executives today, who manage a totally knowledge-based workforce, the only thing that they can do is provide a climate where people can be naturally creative."

> "Mike, how can I create that climate in my firm? In fact, that is one of the primary reasons for my attending this week's program."

> "John, let's dig a little deeper into these Left and Right brain elements that we started out with this morning. Let us step back a little. What was the last major initiative that you embarked upon in the last 5 years within your firm?"

> "Well, in fact we did put in an ERP system," replied John.

> "Tell me John, how did you go about embarking on this project?"

"Being a large scale strategic enterprise-wide project, we did quite a bit of research and planning. We spoke with consultants and potential vendors. Our project lead team visited a few firms – not direct competitors – that had implemented a similar system. Then we picked our vendors and implementers and put in a project plan. Then we set out to execute that strategy. We had clearly allocated budgets, set realistic milestones based on specific tactical outcomes and picked meaningful KPIs for delivery and accountability," said John. His face couldn't hide the fact that he was quite proud of what they had accomplished.

"Congrats! John. Looks like this project was quite successful."

"Oh! Yes, Mike."

"John, were there any mishaps or hiccups along the way? Or was it all executed flawlessly and the process and outcome exactly as your team had predicted?"

"Oh! Mike. What do you think? We are not magicians. Of course, there were several hiccups and set-backs," said John.

"How were these set-backs handled?" asked Mike.

"Well, we put in a lot of time, money and energy to make sure that we got back on track and to be in line with the predicted milestones and outcomes. And this happened a few times along the way" replied John.

"Had you anticipated and accounted for these at the outset of the project?" probed Mike.

"Oh! Of course. Even though we were not always precise, for the most parts it worked out the way we had hoped. As I recall, there were just a couple of surprises; totally unanticipated and it had to do with people's behaviors more than anything else" said John.

"Very good John! You have beautifully described what I call as a complicated project with a good number of uncertainties. Our executives today are trained very well—both in their MBA programs and their managerial experience—to handle this class of problems. While approaching these problems, we first do a STEP environmental scan then followed by SWOT and Value-Chain analysis and then come up with a strategic plan to execute upon. This approach to go into the future is called 'analytical strategy.' This type of traditional strategic planning is just one methodology as to how we approach the future. Analysis before action is the dominant logic of this method. Here we use existing knowledge and analytical models to predict the process and the outcome of the project," said Mike and he paused to take a breath.

"Mike, I am not sure where are you going with this" interjected John, somewhat impatiently.

"This analytical strategy works beautifully and still very relevant when managing *known knowns* and *known unknowns* in both processes and outcome. It is still needed and very applicable during long periods of calm, double-digit growth, generous profits, but punctuated by short periods of turbulence. We call this 'predictive-logic' and you can't get anymore left brained than this. Unfortunately, today's leaders are approaching complex projects—laden with ambiguity and a lot of *unknown unknowns*—with the tools and techniques that only work in complicated and uncertain class of projects. Hence, most analysis that is done prior to taking action is usually wrong or totally misleading, i.e., predictions and trends based on analyzing the wrong variables turn out to be fallacious. When performance does not meet projections a lot of the time, money and energy is spent to get back on to the trend line as you mentioned. Finally, heads roll when the predicted future fails to materialize after repeated failures. Weapons that are purely based on the predictive-logic are totally inadequate for innovation projects fraught with *unknown unknowns*. Unfortunately, executives are approaching innovation, a field that is very dependent on the right brain from a purely left brain perspective," concluded Mike.

"Wow! But Mike, it is precisely this strategic planning technique that I was brainwashed in my MBA program and at every firm that I ever worked. You are now telling me that this way of approaching the future is wrong."

"John, don't feel cheated. This is what is being taught even today in most business schools and still the most widely practiced strategy among firms. I reiterate, it is still a valid way of approaching the future; but works only in a certain class of problems and situations," stressed Mike.

"Yes Mike. I get that. I also get the distinction between risk, uncertainty and ambiguity. So far, you have told me how not to approach innovation. But you haven't told me how to do it. So, what is the approach when there are *unknown unknowns*? How do we make decisions for the future in ambiguous environments" asked John.

Mike began slowly, "Innovators and entrepreneurs don't approach or deal with the *unknown unknowns* in this manner at all. They do not rely on analysis and predictive models alone to take action. Depending on the situation, entrepreneurs tend to use either predictive-logic or creative-logic. In creative-logic, they first take action to create data that does not exist. They tend to think big, think different but start small; usually only with the resources they have on hand. They may start several projects at the same time. They prototype rapidly to test what is real. They establish proof of concept (POC) with the market via quick feedback loops between the voice of demand (VOD), i.e., the market and the voice of supply (VOS), i.e., technology. They uncover unknowns by failing fast, failing cheap and learning quick. They rapidly change direction when reality does not match assumptions. They acquire and pour resources and assets to rapidly scale only when some success materializes, i.e., a proof of concept (POC) is established."

Mike continued, "In summary, in prediction-logic analysis precedes action and in creation-logic action precedes analysis. We call this latter approach to go into the future, emergent strategy." He picked up another napkin to write out some of the steps in emergent strategies and the creation-logic:

> *Think Big, Think Different*
>
> *Start Small, Start Several*
>
> *Prototype Rapidly*
>
> *Fail Fast, Fail Cheap, Fail Smart*
>
> *Learn Quick*
>
> *Proof of Concept = Voice of Demand + Voice of Supply*
>
> *Pour Resources to Scale only after Positive Proof of Concept*
>
> *Celebrate Successes & Celebrate Failures*

John looked at the paper napkin Mike had just handed to him and reflected on both the written text and on Mike's words. He stared at the paper and analyzed the text line by line, trying to transfer that sequence to his reality; picturing the resistance, examples, cases experienced or that could be experienced, and verifying the consistency of the model for his organization.

John started slowly, "I feel that this type of thinking makes sense, but it is completely antithetical to everything I have read, heard or practiced."

In John's response, Mike sensed a little reluctance to believe this emergent strategy and creative-logic argument. So, he took another napkin and started scribbling a few more things.

> "John, you need to look at the emergent strategy and creation-logic with some facts in the background. More than 90% of all innovations start off in the wrong direction. Or for that matter, most innovations start without access to credit, whether the economic times are good or bad. As the consulting firm Innosight's research shows…." he handed John the napkin.

"Yes Mike," said John. "I remember you showed us this data in class today."

> More than 90% of all innovations that ultimately became successful started off in the wrong direction.
>
> Given more money and time, firms are known to pursue the wrong strategies for a longer period of time.
>
> Most new innovations are started without access to credit in good times and bad.

"John, also please remember that a lot of this type of data is very new. It is not widely known among executives."

Again, there was a long pause. Then John spoke again, "Mike, how can I help my executives to overcome the skepticism and fear? How can we learn to apply emergent strategies and the *creation logic?*"

"John, this *creation logic* is not new. We're always using it, although we're not aware of it. In contexts where we move with comfort, we already do the practice carefully, risking no more than necessary. It's like getting started in the do-it-yourself realm. Suppose you get into carpentry. You start with simple repairs, in terms of both their execution and the tools they require. If you fail and you are still interested, you extract learning points. You try again, and probably you acquire new and more sophisticated tools. And once you've known success, you scale your hobby to more complex jobs. Therefore, when we begin to practice in the realm of innovation, the exact same thing occurs. We have to spend a little to learn a lot from our mistakes, prototype rapidly and go step by step to generate small successes and motivate ourselves in the journey until we create that culture of innovation that we're talking about all the time. This is the way to ensure that innovation won't be a high-risk adventure, and that a healthy, stimulating and productive culture of innovation is built. The various processes of innovation must be limited in both time and resources, and must be profitable," Mike concluded.

"Mike, but again, emergent strategies are full of failure. Experimentation is at the heart of this creative-logic. Now, I have to learn to fail and so do my executives, only then will any of my middle management take chances."

"John, you are absolutely right. But, remember, there are several ways to manage it. For instance, you need to separate the people from the project. Teams own projects. Not individuals. Again we need to get back to the basic elements of the right brain components."

"Remember some of the other summaries of the recent studies I showed in class today."

"You mean the studies that show the dismal outcomes of innovation efforts?" asked John.

"Yes, precisely. Do you think any of those results are surprising for me? No. As I said before, executives are approaching innovation with the same left brained hat that they approached every other discipline. Throw in a lot of resources, set up processes and track progress by using a bunch of metrics, i.e., definitions of success. All these elements are necessary but not sufficient. Most of the firms are totally missing out on the critical elements. Having the right enterprise values and creating a climate that encourages entrepreneurial behaviors ultimately determines the success or failure of innovation initiatives. Very few firms are paying attention to the right-brain elements like – Values, Behaviors and Climate."

"Let me summarize. We must break down the elements that comprise the culture of innovation," said Mike as he pulled out one of the sheets he was working on before. On it lay a colorful drawing....

"John, please pay careful attention to these 6 fundamental building blocks of the culture of innovation. The left brain blocks and the right brain blocks are quite self-evident I think. But also, the top four blocks—resources, processes, values and behaviors—are the inputs and the bottom two—success and climate—are outcomes. Every time a firm succeeds, each of the other elements gets reinforced. This reinforcing mechanism happens every time there is a success. Finally, they all get to be intricately intertwined and this is what we call 'culture.'... Let me quickly take you through what each of these stand for."

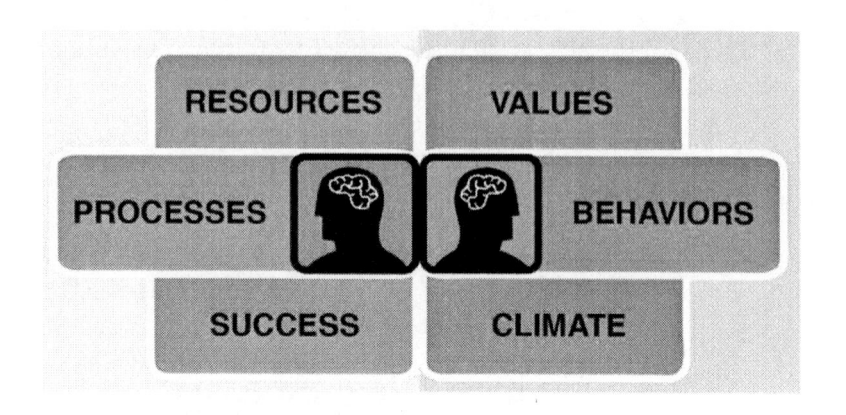

Values of a firm are what we stand for in terms of innovation. What will we fight for? What does the firm fundamentally believe to be true? What are the firm's addictions? They could range from openness, sharing, teamwork, adoring mavericks, and action before analysis. Values are also a firm's moral compass. Usually we can surmise a firm's values by seeing how the firm spends two critical resources—its money and its time.

Resources are how we support our innovation efforts and there are at least seven: 1) Champions – executives who have the desire and understand the importance of innovation within the enterprise and will provide time, space and money for innovation activities; 2) Experts – people who have experience in routinely converting ideas to opportunities and bringing those opportunities to market. They also act as coaches to the talented employees; 3) Talent – the creators, inventors, scientists and idea generators; 4) Systems – the resources that bring together the talent, the experts, the finance, and the processes. This also bridges the external eco-system – suppliers, distributors, market - to the enterprise; 5) Time – to learn, experiment and pursue wild things. Time is usually the scarcest resource within an enterprise. The talent has to get away from their day-to-day activities to focus and pursue very specific growth opportunities; 6) Money – always important to feed innovation. Acknowledging the fact that it can neither be starved nor over-fed; 7) Space—a place to work and play with the ideas and opportunities. Again, separated from the day-to-day cash-cow and continuous improvement activities of the firm.

Behaviors are how we think, approach and act in order to foster innovation. Everyone's – executives and employees. Innovation Behaviors include being opportunistic, flexible, adaptive, collaborative, resilient, taking courageous decisions under uncertainty and dealing with ambiguity. One can learn, practice and coach these behaviors and best of all – no budget needed and no permission required. Above all, please remember that a leader's job is to Energize, Engage and Enable people.

Processes are how do we get innovations done? Creating a funnel to routinely capture ideas; routinely sift ideas from opportunities; and routinely separate the weak from strong opportunities. When opportunities are found, start several small experiments, prototype rapidly, fail fast, fail cheap, fail smart and finally, move to scale-up quickly when a golden jewel is found.

Climate is what is it like to work in this firm? Is the company climate favorable to innovation? It is vibrant, and one that cultivates passion, stimulates and challenges people to take chances, fosters learning and reflection and doesn't squash independent thinking. The best test for climate is to ask the question, "are people excited to come to work every day?"

Success is how we measure our innovation output. What does success mean inside our firm? How is success measured—process and outcome? How are we rewarded? Do we tolerate mistakes? Are learning, experimentation, failure and feedback rewarded? Measures of success determine our behaviors and processes. When we feel successful, our environment, values, processes and behaviors get reinforced. Repeated success leads to further reinforcement of these principles and over time all these elements get integrated and at times ossified and that is *culture*!

John was surprised by the simplicity of the model, and by the logic that supported it. It was one of those things that made one wonder why he hadn't arrived at the same reasoning on his own. In short, he felt that the model was obvious.

There was a long silence.

> "Mike, I know you said this before. You say that culture is an outcome. But, isn't culture an input? Isn't it a given for any firm? Isn't it what it is?"

> "John, culture is an outcome of success. Let me give you an example."

> "Suppose you work for a nascent, small start-up. In the early stages of the firm, there is no culture. However, there are the values and behaviors of the founders. Suppose for instance that nobody is buying their products or services. Then, it is quite natural for this start-up to change their approach or processes and/or even behaviors. Still, nobody is buying their wares. So, again the firm will probably change the way it does things. They are flexible and agile. Let us suppose that after a few times, suddenly a few customers show interest in the firm's product, i.e. they have had their first success. What do you think that the people in the firm will do next?"

> "Oh! Mike, obviously they will again try out the processes and behaviors and the set of resources that lead them to their first success after all."

> "Precisely. They will repeat the things that they did last that led them to success. Only now more customer line up to buy the product or service. What happens then?"

> "Well, they will now think that they have gotten a winning formula and the firm will reuse the formula," responded John in an eager voice.

"Bravo John! Now do you realize how the six fundamental building blocks get entrenched and get burnt into the firm's DNA over time due to the repeated reinforcement of each of the elements that is moderated by success each time? And what do we call that?"

"Culture!" retorted John quite enthusiastically.

Following this exchange, John seemed to be pensive. Mike was enjoying the hiatus and relaxed a bit by again sipping on his wine. Mike believed that he had made quite a bit of progress with John. But John felt otherwise. While he liked a lot of the concepts that Mike had explained, deep inside, John was still not convinced. Something was still gnawing at him. The entire discussion thus far seemed too obvious and all too clear. It sounded too simplistic for the ever-doubting and skeptical John. He just did not want to be taken for a ride by a somewhat learned snake-oil salesman.

Again, after several minutes of pondering John wanted to be firm but at the same time respectful and so he spoke haltingly, "Mike, innovation is much more complex than what you make it out to be............I don't believe it is so obvious........ It is way too simplistic for my liking.......I am not sure.....er"

"Ay! Ay! John. Great thinking." Mike interrupted John; as though he was expecting this any moment. This reaction again took John by surprise. Mike quickly started looking around. He seemed to be looking at the top of the buildings or towards some trees nearby. He then quickly excused himself from the table and walked towards what seemed like a tall tree that was just on the other side of a small parking lot. Within a minute or so, Mike returned with a nice sized pine cone in his hand and asked, "John, do you like the shape of this pine cone?"

"Oh! Yes, Mike, it is a beautiful cone."

"John, do you think this is a simple or a complex structure?"

"Mike, it is obviously complex; what are you trying to get at Mike?"

"John, do you realize how it became so complex and beautiful?"

In a flash it came back flooding to John. A few months ago, he had seen his young son do a class project on Fibonacci sequence and its prevalence in nature – in beautiful sea-shell patterns, flowers and fruits and plants. He quickly retorted, "It is the Fibonacci. I got your point Mike. Likewise simple Tessellations and Fractals also give rise to beautiful and complex shapes."

"Righto John! So are complex disciplines. Most forms of western music is created from seven notes. One of the most complex structure known to man—the DNA—is made up of 5 basic elements; Carbon, Oxygen, Hydrogen, Nitrogen and Phosphorous. All of mathematics is made up of two basic operations and so is everything digital. Complexity can only be explained through great simplicity. You need to break complexity into its fundamental building blocks, only then will you understand complex systems. One should always try to understand and uncover the elemental or foundational building blocks of complex systems."

John seemed to have ignited something in Mike. Mike moved to the edge of the chair and towards John and looked straight into his eyes and continued in somewhat of a terse manner, "academia, consultants, politicians, government workers and all experts—lawyers, tax accountants, engineers, doctors—love to make things complex. Firstly, it gives them a chance to look intellectual. Secondly, and probably more likely, it is a way of protecting one's job. So, in general, humans like to complicate things. They love to provide complex solutions to solve complex problems. However, in order to understand anything rather deeply, one must approach the issue simply. In that simplicity you will discover beauty."

Mike eased back into the chair like a boxer would return to his chair, after winning a round. But John wouldn't give up that easily. He had had years of experience grilling and exposing the shallowness of smooth-talking, buzz-word compliant consultants and buzz-word creating academics. However this non-descript unknown professor seemed to be pushing John's abilities to separate good from grime. He wasn't convinced yet.

This time the recess was quite long but John's poker face did not reveal his discomfort. He again slowly and quietly began, "Mike, recall Re-Engineering, recall Balanced Scorecard, recall EVA. These were all fads. Don't you think the current hoopla about Innovation is a fad? I am all the time bombarded by consultants and academics trying to sell me innovation stuff. The books, the software, the methodologies are all exploding. Don't you think that this too shall pass?"

Mike gave the same smug smile again; the one that John didn't like and he started "John, you have every right to make sure that you are not jumping on to a temporary bandwagon. I totally agree that consultants and academics don't help themselves. There are a few things that you need to keep in mind about management disciplines, principles, concepts and tools. Firstly, Strategy, Marketing, Finance, Operations, etc. are all disciplines. Within each discipline you have principles, concepts and tools. What you will notice is that disciplines are more enduring than principles, principles are more enduring than concepts and concepts are more enduring than tools. For instance, in the early stages of the quality movement the dominant concept was error detection and the dominant tool was sampling. After a while, this concept was super-ceded by quality assurance where the dominant tool was error prevention. So, it is usually the concepts and tools that go through cycles and fads."

Mike continued, "Secondly, Innovation is a discipline. All disciplines have a fundamental objective; a profound purpose. The fundamental objective of Accounting is to keep score of all the firm's activities. The primary purpose of Innovation is to create new products, services, markets, business models or a culture that will radically change the competitive game in your favor. Specifically, the objective of creating a Culture of Innovation is timeless; the only one that gives you the most sustainable advantage over time."

"Thirdly, some of the fundamental principles of creating a climate where people are naturally creative and great opportunities are captured have not changed in over 500 years. During the renaissance in Italy, Lorenzo de Medici had brought together painters, sculptors, philosophers, architects, builders, scientists, and writers to create a breeding ground for new ideas. In the late 18th century and early 19th century, coffeehouses were hotbeds of innovation and experimentation. In London, coffeehouses gave rise to new business models in insurance, lottery, joint-stock companies and new discoveries in science. In Paris, they were the hives of activity for political discontent as well as the latest in art and literature. The Viennese cafes gave rise to new thought movements like positivism and psychology—Freud's Wednesday salon at Berggstrasse—and new art forms like Klimt's Secession movement. In the early 20th century, Edison had brought together a highly select group of diverse experts – a mechanical assistant from England, a mathematician, a Swiss clockmaker, a German glassblower, carpenters, machinists and general laboratory helpers – to his Menlo Park invention factory in New Jersey. This is not different from what goes on today in Bangalore, Shanghai, Silicon Valley, Singapore and Tel-Aviv," Mike finished and slowly eased back into his chair.

Chapter 6

Starting the Journey

Their wine glasses were empty.

> "John, it's about time we got back, I don't think there are too many stars left to come out. I suggest you put away all these notes and let all the information we've put on the table—both literally and figuratively—settle."

Mike arranged the napkins and papers in the order in which they'd appeared and placed them before John like a valuable present. It was true that they'd gone over a lot in a very short period of time, and he needed to digest it and convert it into something applicable.

They asked the waiter for the check. Even though John was exhausted he wanted to know more about Mike, "Mike, what is it about teaching that attracts you?"

Mike leaned back in his chair again. He was a born conversationalist; if you asked him a question, a world opened up before him.

"Oh! John, I am not good at anything else!" The two of them laughed heartily and Mike clapping his hands as he always does when he laughs out loud.

Mike continued, "No John; seriously, I love the academic environment. You are all the time exposed to incredible people who are leading and managing firms globally; solving very difficult problems and trying to make a difference in people's lives. In fact, today, *Management* is the most widespread philosophy on earth. It is not any religion, but it is *Management*. Management, the principles of management and the ubiquitous practice of management in all spheres of life touches the most number of people and effects almost the entire planet. So, as someone who teaches management, I have to be very careful and take very seriously what I say and what I profess in front of leaders and managers."

"John, to tell you the truth, I have never worked a day in my life. I have never had a real job. I have been a student and an academic all my life. I guess I just love to learn."

Again, John liked Mike's observation about management. More so, he could not believe that Mike had no real-world work experience. But, before he could say anything, Mike continued, "I learn a lot when I am in the class, especially a room full of executives and managers. Believe me John, there are few original thoughts in my head or novel words in my mouth that somehow have not been influenced by some great person or put there by some true genius. All I do is look, listen and learn the best ideas, concepts and tools that are around me and see how I may be able to package it and present it in a way that will take the vast audience—that I have been blessed with—from clutter to clarity. So, I learn best when I teach."

"Aaaerr...... in fact John, all of us are like that. We humans learn best when one has to teach something—a concept or skill—to another person" said Mike.

Being a very good auditory learner, John was again intrigued by the very last comment. Also, by now, he knew that Mike dropped these types of statements all the time; statements that at first blush either made no sense or was blindingly profound. So he quickly said, "Mike, what do you mean?"

Just then the waiter came back with John's credit card and thanked them for dining with them and bid them both a great evening. Mike got up as John put away the credit card and receipt and started to gather all the notes and paper. He had somehow managed to keep all of them in the order in which Mike's ideas were flowing.

Quickly, Mike took all the notes and paper from John's hand and mixed them all up and handed it back to John.

> "Mike, why did you do that for?" cried John. "Is this another one of your teaching techniques? If so, it's not funny. Do you know how long it's going to take me to decipher your code, let alone translate it into my business?" His raised voice clearly expressed his surprise at Mike's frivolous act.

> "Precisely John. Trust me with this one. Please, humor me. In fact you will thank me for this later on. Anyway why do you have to worry; I am just a phone call or a Skype call away."

> John quickly cooled down and as he got up he sarcastically asked: "How do we get back to the residence building, Socratic Professor?"

> "Oh! No! Please don't address me as professor. It's way too much of a responsibility; if you know what I mean. I am as much a student as you are. Please call me Mike."

> "Alright Mike," said John. While he was curious, he did not want to follow up on the responsibility comment that

Mike just made. This then would distract Mike away from the previous comment that he was yet to complete. Again, it was one of those deep thoughts that he would have to get back to and ruminate at a later time.

The two of them awkwardly stumbled towards the town square; the after effects of all the food and wine.

"Let's see," said Mike, standing in the middle of the square. "Now, when we reach the outskirts of town, we'll have two options for returning. We can either walk through the stand of elms along the same path that brought us here, or we can take the path that runs along the right side of the road and is little longer."

Mike started walking without waiting for a response. John went on in silence. They were coming to the edge of town, and it seemed that Mike had ended up choosing the path that ran parallel with the highway.

John meditated as they walked, hands clasped behind his back and his eyes turned towards Mike; hoping that Mike would pick up the train of thought that got started when they were interrupted by the waiter. Seemed like Mike needed a nudge to get back into the discussion. John broke the ice by asking, "So Mike, tell me why do we learn best when we teach others something; a concept or skill."

"Ah! I am sorry John. I rarely forget to get back to a comment or question. I guess I must be tired."

"No apology necessary Mike, in fact, I am the one that should be apologizing for the non-stop barrage of questions."

"Probably it's the notes shuffling incident that threw me off," said Mike laughingly. John reciprocated.

"Ah! Actually it's my turn to ask you a question. Tell me

John, are you a reader? Do you read a lot of newspapers, magazines and/or books?"

"Are you kidding? Do you think I can afford not to. I read like crazy. Unfortunately, I wish I had more time to read non-business stuff. But I am so overwhelmed just trying to keep abreast with what is going in the business world, I have no time for the real fun stuff."

"John, you are not alone. Most executives are like that. In fact most readers are like that. For a moment forget about all the day-to-day general news and knowledge that you need to know; but let us focus on all the business articles and books that you read constantly. How much of what you read do you really remember; let alone use?"

John fell silent. The silence made itself felt; only their footsteps could be heard on the asphalt as well as the hum from the nearby freeway. Mike waited for a response as he turned towards John who had fallen a step behind him. As though he was expecting the answer, Mike reassured John, "don't worry John, be candid."

John almost felt ashamed and asked, "Why is it Mike? Why is it that I don't put to use what I know and what I learn? And, and, please tell me that I am not alone."

"Oh! John. Don't worry; you are not alone. Most people are like that. I used to be like that. In fact, it was an executive in one of my classes who suggested that I read a book about it and that changed my life. Forever. Please remind me via an email to send you a link to that book."

"All the data and information that we are constantly either being bombarded with or we ourselves voluntarily imbibing is not really knowledge. For the most part we believe that most of it is just not pertinent to our lives and our businesses. Even if you feel that it may be useful, we will find excuses to reject them by saying, ah! our business is different, or it will not work in my part of the world or that these are somehow different circumstances. It is human nature to think and feel that we are all unique and that we are all different. So, all of us around the world, we focus more on our differences while in fact there is way more commonality among all of us than we realize or want to acknowledge. So, we tend to reject all ideas and concepts until and unless we have direct firsthand experience. That is precisely the reason why most people who attend seminars and conferences do not act upon new information," emphasized Mike.

Mike continued, "However, if you see that the information perfectly fits with what you are currently wrestling then, it is at this moment that what was previously just data and information gets converted into knowledge. And, knowledge triggers thinking and reflection. Again, this is what you are experiencing currently. You came to this program having thought deeply about the issues you are facing. Only then will you start to believe in the concepts and ideas; even though you have had prior exposure to it and probably several times. Even after the first-hand experience, those beliefs get grounded, refined and solidified only when you reflect upon the experience and start to relate them or teach others about your experiences or skills. That is real learning. That is why story-telling and coaching is such an important component of leading change. Change will never happen unless you learn."

Again there was this protracted pause. "Mike, wow. Hmmm! Are you trying to tell me that I need to teach whatever I have learned this week to my leadership team?"

> "Bingo John! Bingo! Please remember that, if you decide to embark upon this journey, you are going to be the CEO: Chief Evangelist Officer. Get it! CEO!" And they both start laughing.

"John, if you don't believe, there is no way you can convince others to follow. If you don't believe, please don't start the journey."

"Oh My God! Mike. You cunning creature." John slapped Mike's shoulder in jest. He took the liberty of doing so, because he was confident that he was at least a couple of years older than Mike.

John seemed to have had an epiphany and Mike was grinning as he waited for John to continue.

"Mike, now I understand why you shuffled the notes. Wow, errrr....you want me to labor over it, struggle with it, make sense out of it, put it in my own order, believe it and tell a story to my executive team."

Mike listened with pleasure to his new friend, who had just had an insight. Again, he was impressed that John was a very fast learner. Most importantly, Mike respected John for his open mind, keen questioning and wanting to learn. Also, Mike seemed very content with himself; feeling a sense of accomplishment.

And this was followed by a long pregnant pause. The path took them quite close to the noisy freeway and the ugly concrete. John did not like this path; especially after having walked through the beautiful stand of elms earlier in the evening.

Within a couple of minutes, the path had turned away from the freeway, the noise was gone and the path had led them into an expansive meadow patch on a small hillock. Mike was looking up at the sky when he said, "isn't it marvelous." John was also soaking up the open sky above. It was full of stars; way more than what he normally gets to see from the city. Many many more. It was made even more beautiful by the moon-less night.

John now realized why Mike had set out on this path without even waiting for a response. Again, it seemed like one more of Mike's pre-meditated machinations – walking through the gigantic elm alley during sunlight and walking back through the mighty meadow under the open starry sky.

John's view of Mike had changed dramatically in a short span of time. Mike had surprised John with his inexhaustible repertoire of stories, sayings, schemas and scheming. His reservations had turned to respect.

They walked the rest of the way in silence, each occupied with his own thoughts. When they could see the school buildings John renewed the conversation, "Mike how can I ever thank you for this evening?"

Mike remained silent. He kept walking till they came to the edge of the meadow and stopped the path split into two. "John, if you come upon a fork in the road….." before Mike could complete the sentence, John shouted "Take It!……Yogi Berra." The two of them started roaring with laughter and high-fived.

When the guffaw had died down, "Well, now you know why I didn't hesitate to extend our conversation," said Mike.

They had arrived at the front courtyard of the residence hall. Even though it was quite late, groups of executives could be seen through the big windows of the bar chatting away merrily. Also, the walk through the meadow and the fresh air seemed to have revived both Mike and John. John felt that he should capitalize on this sudden boost of energy and bring up an issue that probably Mike had forgotten. Towards the end of the lunch break, Mike had asked John to go back and look for the classical root of the word discipline. So, he gently broached the topic.

> "Mike, you had said that you use the word discipline in at least four ways. So, far I seem to have understood it quite well from three perspectives – field of study, deliberate and determined. My research tells me that the classical meaning of the word discipline comes from old French

descipline, desciple and that comes from the Latin word disciplina that stands for "instruction" and discipulus that means "pupil". And the root for all these words is discere, i.e., "to learn". So, discipline is about learning to know, acquire, or become acquainted with. You seemed to have alluded to this learning in passing throughout this evening. Could you please shed some light on this specific meaning of discipline?"

"Good work John! You don't fail to amaze me. I don't mean to ingratiate you or try to boost your ego. I am sure others have told you this before. You are a very fast learner. A very good student." As Mike spoke, John could clearly notice a surprise in Mike's eye brows even in the dim light of the evening.

Mike quickly glanced at his watch and it was a quarter to eleven. As he started speaking, he then slowly inched towards the stone sitting bench next to the garden entrance of the building; with John a step behind but clearly paying attention.

"John, you are asking the central question as to why some firms survive while most of them die."

Hearing this unexpected answer, John quickly moved and stood in front of Mike as Mike sat down on the bench. I don't not want to miss any of this he thought to himself as Mike continued, "The Chinese philosopher Confucius defined three methods by which we learn wisdom: first, by reflection, which is noblest; second, by imitation, which is easiest; and third by experience; which is the bitterest. The first method, while important, is very slow. The second method, imitation, is by far the most widely used method for any learning activity; the basic idea of a school rests on this idea. Imitation is by definition based on existing knowledge. For instance, reading books, listening to experts and studying cases are all using existing knowledge."

John was as little perplexed as to where Mike was going with this and how it is related to the existence and survival of firms. But he did not interrupt.

> "In order to understand, practice and be disciplined in our innovation activities, we have to fully grasp the intricacies and inter-relationships between two very important concepts – knowledge and learning. When involved in innovation activities, a firm could move forward either by using existing knowledge to take action or take action to discover new knowledge. Put in another way, the former is analysis before action and the latter is action before analysis. Unfortunately, in a majority of firms today, still the predominant logic is to depend on existing knowledge to execute innovation projects. However, innovation is about dealing with 'unknown unknowns' and existing knowledge is either grossly inadequate or using it simply lead to fallacious assumptions and thus wrong predictions of the future. This is where a firm has to learn through 'experience.' The only way one learns the hidden underlying unknown variables is through action, i.e., by applying the creation logic."

"Mike, I get the distinction. We did discuss some of this before. But, what is this to do with either survival or death of firms?"

"Patience my friend. Please bear with me for a while. These are some of the hardest concepts to get our heads around. So, please don't worry if you don't absorb it all tonight. I'll plant a few seeds now and you need to slowly ruminate on these."

"Here is the problem. Knowledge is an obstacle to innovation. Knowledge is our accumulated wisdom. As mentioned before, it is accrued through all the three modes of learning – imitation, experience and reflection.

There is no doubt that knowledge is extremely useful for us to function and act—cross the street, operate a machine and earn a living. It is also this knowledge through which we perceive everything around us—accept, reject, judge, evaluate and conform to a pattern. It is our existing and accrued knowledge that conditions us, shapes our thoughts and becomes the filter through which we see the world. On the other hand, knowledge also blinds us from accepting new ideas and opportunities. So, in many ways knowledge is like culture. It has value in certain situations and is absolutely of no value in others."

"Knowledge is about the 'known' world. Learning is about the 'unknown' world. There are several psychological tests to show that existing knowledge blocks discovery and creativity. So, existing knowledge relegates us to imitation and comparison. After all, imitation is doing what has worked for others and hope that it will work as well when adopted by you. So, knowledge moves us away from freedom. Let us go back to the Latin root of the word discipline—to learn. The act of learning is the act of discipline. If we have a desire or a constant quest to learn then we cannot conform to existing knowledge. If we conform we cannot learn. So, a disciplined mind is free of conformity."

"Here is the catch. For the most part, society punishes, i.e., disciplines, us for not conforming. But the learning mind has the discipline not to conform. It is a mind that seeks freedom. A disciplined mind does not imitate, follow or obey. So, discipline gives you freedom. Discipline is freedom. Where there is conformity, there is comparison. The entire field of Quality and 6-sigma is about comparison and conformance to a pre-determined or 'known' standard. On the other hand, freedom means to live without comparison, without competition. You recognize innovation when you see it, because it has no comparison!"

"We have already discussed this before. Radical innovation and radical change is not possible without the negation or undoing of existing knowledge. To learn is to be disciplined. But to constantly learn, we must accept the fact that we don't know what we don't know, i.e., unconscious incompetence, all the time. Innovation happens only when there is new learning. A learning that is unique to your experience. An experience that you have adventured to learn by taking action. Not living through others' experiences or knowledge. Not by imitating others."

The lights from the nearby by corridor was good enough. So, Mike pulled out a napkin from his pant pocket. As Mike was writing, John stood laughing and he commented, "Mike! Do you carry these all the time?"

"Yep. One can never tell when one would run into a potential student or a victim who really wants to learn," joked Mike. And the two of them laughed.

```
        ┌──→ Unconscious Incompetence
        │         │
        │         ↓   Discipline 1
        │             (Knowledge)
        │     Conscious Incompetence
        │         │
  Discipline 4    ↓   Discipline 2
  (Learning)          (Purposeful Practice)
        ↑     Conscious Competence
        │         │
        │         ↓   Discipline 3
        │             (Perseverance & Grit)
        └──── Unconscious Competence
```

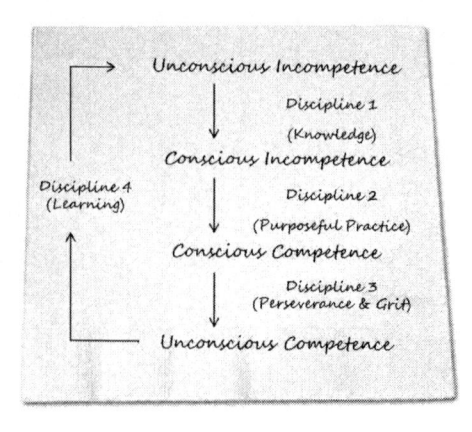

John seemed a little perplexed. He was under the impression that unconscious competence was a state that firms would love to be at. So, this new arrow that sent the firm back to unconscious incompetence was a little disturbing for him. He slowly asked Mike, "Please help me out here. I am not sure I fully grasp this."

"When we are learning a new language one is totally open to what is being said by the teacher. There is complete concentration towards the mood, the emotion and the motions. There is total attention and sensitivity. In essence the mind does not suppress anything. The mind is completely quiet and judgment free. That is when learning happens. This should not be any different than when you are observing or listening to an existing customer or to potential customers. That is when deep understanding and empathy happens. That is discipline. This total and undivided attention results in new learning and that in turn leads to innovation."

"Unfortunately, this rarely happens. We all succumb to our own existing knowledge. Our heads are full of beliefs, conclusions, appraisals, and categorizations. We rarely listen to the facts. Most of us listen with our own minds chattering and we are not actually listening. To listen actually, the mind must be extraordinarily quiet and silent. That is learning. The very act of learning is discipline. Learning happens only when there is humility and passion. The humility to acknowledge that I don't know what I don't know, i.e., unconscious incompetence, and the passion to discover new things, inquire and be curious to solve things. So, in summary, innovation happens when we are humble. This is true for individuals as well. In order for us to change, we have to undo what we know. We all know very well the effects of not changing; you land up as a statistic among all the dead firms. That is why innovation is a journey and not a destination. This cycle never ends."

"Mike, what you are saying is that Innovation is about pure learning. What you are saying is that firms survive because of continuous learning. So, Innovation is continuous learning."

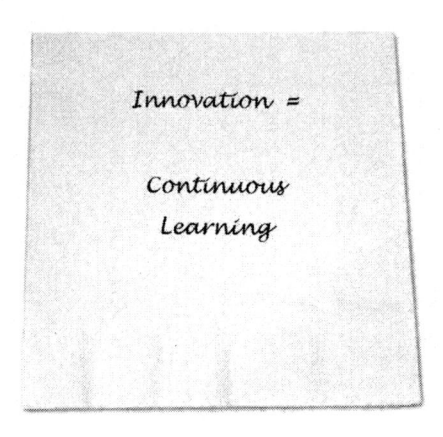

> *Innovation =*
>
> *Continuous Learning*

"You are right on the mark John. Survival is about the rate at which firms learn about their changing environment. Yes, Innovation is continuous learning."

Like many times before this evening, there was this long gap as John pondered the implications of this latest paper napkin. Mike could hear a small gasp from John as he said, "Wow Mike! That means that we as a firm have to first learn how to learn. Oh! please don't tell me I am opening another Pandora's Box."

"You are John. But as long as you recognize what you need to learn, that itself is a great step forward."

This was much deeper than John had ever expected. He had not equated Innovation to *learning* and that to the very survival of the firm. He stood in silence rocking back and forth for several minutes with the note in his hand. The day had turned out to be wilder than he could ever imagine. He looked at his watch and it was nearing midnight and he felt guilty for having kept Mike for that long.

"Mike, tomorrow I am leaving early in the morning. The respite will be over. And you can be sure that I'll turn over your theory of the culture of innovation many times in my head."

"It's a bit more than just a theory, John," said Mike, raising his index finger to reinforce his point and continued. "Next Monday, John, when you're back in your office, remember the fork in the road and remember the episode from *Alice in Wonderland*. And remember that when you're faced with a journey you want to undertake, it does not matter which path you take. There are many roads to heaven. Just make sure you pave it with entrepreneurial values, encourage innovative behaviors, provide resources to set up processes for routinely taking ideas and converting them into opportunities in a sand-box you have roughly defined. John, go ahead and create a climate, a safe sand-box or a park, where people can be naturally creative. Don't worry about success, it will surely follow. And most importantly, remember it is a journey and not a destination. Make sure everyone enjoys the journey."

"I'll definitely think about all of that Mike. Remember, that I now need to create a lecture for my executive team. Mike, thank you so much for this evening. You have no idea how very grateful I am for your time, your patience with this poor anxious student and your company."

"Oh, no, no! Someone told me once that among friends no thanks are in order, and I think that's a splendid statement."

"All right Mike."

"John, be passionate, be disciplined and be humble. That way, you can master any discipline. Good luck on your journey, my friend. And good night."

"Good night, Mike."

Mike handed one last post-it note to John. John opened it as Mike turned and walked away.

> *Innovation*
>
> Reveals the "Unknown"
> Redefines the "Known"
> Renovates the "Worn."

Authors

Jay Rao is a Professor at Babson College in Boston.

His research and consulting focus is in the areas of: Innovation Strategy - Culture of Innovation - Innovation Implementation and Scaling - Strategies for Innovation and Growth - Service Strategies and Customer Experience Innovation - Corporate Entrepreneurship.

Through Babson Executive Education he has taught for BBVA, Fresinius Medical Care, Covidien, BAE Systems, Novartis, Ocean Spray, U.S. Navy, SABIC, Citizens Bank, Merck, Masco Corp., Scottish Enterprise, EMC, GlaxoSmithKline, and others. He has also taught executives and/or consulted for Verti, Reed Elsevier, PWC, Bayer Material Science, Iberdrola, Assa Abloy Americas, Massachusetts General Hospital, Banco Occidente, Chilectra, Agricola Garces, Groupo Security, Entel, Coagra, Inter-American Development Bank, EMDSerono, Lojack, Fidelity Investments, Merrill Lynch, Boston Scientific Corporation and others. He is a frequent speaker at trade conferences and enterprise retreats.

He is a member of the Innovation Advisory Board at Ocean Spray. He has a family business background and a board member of the HJKP Trust.

Mail: raoj@babson.edu
Blog: http://innovationatwork.wordpress.com/

Fran Chuán is an Entrepreneur.

A former Engineer fascinated by the potential latent in human attitudes.

His passion to do things different and innovate it took him, after 25 years as Manager in diverse Multinationals and countries, to found Dícere (2004), a consultancy specializing in people, stimulating the entrepreneurship we all have inside us, and generating as a consequence sustainable innovation.

He develops his activity with companies like Repsol, BBVA, Novartis, Verti, Reckitt Benckiser, Danone Group, among others, as a broad number of SME.

Is Member of various Advisory Boards.

Collaborates with institutions like Babson, IESE and Laureate International University.

Mail: fchuan@dicere.es
Web: www.dicere.es
Blog: http://dicere-wakab.net/